VICTOROLOGY

Say goodbye to spiritual frustration and live the overcomer's life

SCOTT NEWTON SMITH

Published by

Scott Newton Smith Ministries, Inc.

1250 Scenic Hwy S

1701-166

Lawrenceville GA 30045

First Edition

TABLE OF CONTENTS

DEDICATION

*This book is dedicated to Scarlet, my best
friend, sweetheart, and the unwavering
light behind my journey in ministry.
Nearly three decades of marriage have shown
me the depth of your love, patience, and
encouragement as I traveled and preached
the truths now inscribed in these pages.
You have been my home amidst my wanderings,
my cheerleader through every challenge, and the
silent force that has propelled me forward.
For every sacrifice made and every moment of support
given, this book is as much yours as it is mine.
I love you.*

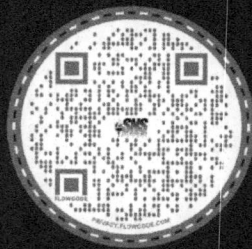

INTRODUCTION

My promise to you as you read this book is this:

This book will help you say goodbye to spiritual frustration and live the overcomer's life.

First, a story:

Two fellows went an elk hunting expedition in the deep northwestern United States. They chartered a pilot to fly them up in a small plane, land them in the northwestern wilds, and let them hunt for three days, after which he would return to pick them up. When the pilot dropped them off, he said, "Look, this plane is only going to hold three elk. Three elk is the max. Any more than three will have to be left here."

Well, three days later, he comes back, and these guys drag four elk out of the woods that they killed over during the hunt. They started to load them onto the plane, but the pilot stopped them in their tracks. "No, no. I told you that you could only bring three elk. You can't bring four elk. The plane won't take off with more than you, me, and three elk."

The two guys then proceeded to argue with him, saying, "Listen, the pilot that brought us in here last year had the same kind of plane you have; it was the same everything. He said the same thing to us, too, but we got four elk on that plane, and the plane took off."

The pilot was surprised, replying, "Wait a minute. You're telling me that a pilot that brought you in here last year let you put four elk on the plane, and the plane took off?"

They responded eagerly, "Yes, that's right."

"Okay, then," the pilot conceded, "we'll put the four elk on the plane."

So they put the four elk on the plane, and the plane started down the little dirt runway; it sputtered and spat but eventually lifted off the ground, rising to a few hundred feet—before promptly descending into a nosedive and crashing.

The two hunters crawled out of the wreckage, and one of them looked at the other and said, "Where do you think we are?"

His friend looked around and said, "Looks to me like about the same place we crashed last year."

That funny story represents the experience of too many Christians.

Living from crash to crash, crisis to crisis, unable to maintain altitude in their walk with Jesus, even in their overall Christian life.

Do you feel like that?

- Maybe you feel overwhelmed by life's challenges.
- Maybe you lack a deep sense of purpose and identity.
- Maybe financial, relational, or spiritual stress is frequent in your life.
- Maybe you struggle to maintain faith during tough times, feeling isolated and without support.
- Maybe you feel you lack spiritual discipline or just live spiritually dry.
- Maybe you feel your life is marked more by uncertainty and a longing for something more fulfilling and grounded than what you currently experience.

If any of that is you, then you're reading the right book.

The principles laid out in *Victorology* are far more than theoretical musings; they're battle-tested strategies forged in the realities of life's toughest moments. These truths have been lived out in my own journey, where I've experienced firsthand their transformative power.

But it doesn't stop there.

Through extensive study and observation, I've seen these same principles revolutionize the lives of countless Christians, demonstrating a universal applicability that transcends individual circumstances.

The principles you'll find here in *Victorology* aren't man-made ideas; they're divine truths, provided by God in His inerrant, infallible scriptures, given to draw us closer to Him, to know Him deeply, and to enjoy Him fully.

For over three decades I have traveled the country and the world, committed to communicating life principles through this lens: Scripture is our ultimate guide for a life that pleases God and fulfills our deepest desires. It's this solid grounding that ensures the reliability and effectiveness of every insight shared in the book.

Over decades of ministry, I've had the privilege of preaching these truths to thousands. The response has been overwhelmingly affirming—a constant stream of emails, direct messages, letters, and cards from individuals whose lives have been dramatically changed. These aren't just casual acknowledgments; they're heartfelt testimonies of paradigm shifts and profound life transformations. People speak of newfound joy, purpose, and a deep-seated peace that comes from living in alignment with God's Word.

Victorology isn't just a book; it's a testimony to the power of God's truth in action. As you absorb these powerful paradigms, you can expect:

- Insightful teachings and practical applications for everyday challenges.
- Inspirational (and often humorous) stories and biblical references to guide and strengthen faith.
- A step-by-step guide to embracing and living out the victorious life designed for each believer.

The result for you will be that you will gain:

- Deep understanding of your identity in Christ, enhancing self-worth and spiritual resilience.
- Strategies for aligning finances with biblical principles, promoting stewardship and generosity.
- Insights on utilizing spiritual warfare weapons and biblical mindsets which strengthen faith in adversity.
- Guidance on enduring trials with perseverance and joy, cultivating a steadfast spirit that delivers growth and impact regardless of circumstances.
- Principles for living a pure life, focusing on long-term spiritual rewards over immediate gratification.

The Westminster Catechism begins with the question, *"What is the chief end (purpose) of man?"*

The answer is: *"To glorify God and enjoy Him forever."*

If nothing else, I am confident that this book will assist you in accomplishing that end for your own life.

Let's go!

CHAPTER 0
THIS BOOK WON'T WORK FOR YOU, UNLESS...

The chapter number is not a typo. In order for this book to work for you personally, you have to be functioning at a certain basic level as a Christian. Fundamentals matter.

While each chapter in this book contains powerful, life-altering strategies, they rest on the same success foundations as it pertains to Christian living that have been in place since the book of Acts was written.

There are *basics* in the Christian life that you can't shortcut any more than you can shortcut putting gas in your tank if you expect your car to get you anywhere at all.

Someone asked Charles Spurgeon once, "What's more important, prayer or bible reading?" To which Spurgeon replied with his own question: "What's more important, breathing in, or breathing out?"

You can't get running, jumping and flying to work if breathing hasn't been mastered to some healthy degree!

This book is designed to speak into the lives of those who have already trusted Christ as their Lord and Savior.[1] This means that a desire to walk the path of spiritual fitness exists in them, i.e.

---

1. If you don't fit in that category, and you are either, 1) not sure you are a Christian, or, 2) know for a fact you have *never* become a Christ-follower and been "born again" as Jesus talked about, and you need to take the first step, then go NOW to the Appendix of this book. I have something very special for you there.

engaging daily with God through prayer, Bible study, and active involvement in their local church.

These are the basics. And to the degree you implement these, the advanced strategies will work. In some cases, the advanced strategies in this book will *also* help you work your basics even better.

Sometimes a coach has to confront his team at halftime. He'll stand in front of them with a ball and bat in his hand, and say, *"Okay, fellas. Pay attention... THIS is a ball! THIS is a bat!"*

Our effectiveness on the field is only as good as our mastery of the basics.

Having said that, to the degree you struggle in the basics, there are principles in this book that will help you master them even more. But the heart of any strategy toward victorious living must always hold the basics in high regard throughout.

For further clarification, let's briefly outline these "basics," providing a foundation for the victorious Christian life we aspire to live.

1. **Daily Prayer**: Have a consistent prayer life that serves as the backbone of your relationship with God. This dialogue with the God who made you is your lifeline, through which you seek His direction, express gratitude, and renew personal peace.

2. **Bible Study**: Engage with the Bible on a daily basis, seeking to understand its teachings and apply its wisdom to your life. This isn't just reading; it's a deep, meditative practice that shapes your worldview and actions.

3. **Church Involvement**: You are not a solitary Christian. Community is important, so regularly participate in your local church through worship, fellowship, and service, recognizing that we are all parts of one body in Christ.

4. **Spiritual Disciplines**: Beyond prayer and scripture study,

you practice of other spiritual disciplines such as service and stewardship, understanding that these practices deepen your faith and discipline your desires.

If any of this sounds intimidating, I'm going to help with that right now.

As a matter of fact, you may be thinking already: *"But, Scott, that's why I bought this book! These are the first struggles I think of when I consider how defeated I feel!"*

Here's the fact: reconnecting with God after a time of long lapse *is not hard and anyone can do it*. Even if you just commit to ten minutes a day to start, well… that's not nothing!

But in case you need it here is a spiritual jump-start sequence.

A QUICK TUTORIAL ON RECONNECTING WITH GOD

If you find yourself drifting or disconnected from God, take heart. Reconnecting with Him is this simple:

1. **Acknowledge**: Begin by acknowledging your need for God and your desire to reconnect. This simple act of humility opens the door to His presence.
2. **Confess**: Confess any known sin, knowing that God is faithful and just to forgive us and cleanse us from all unrighteousness (1 John 1:9).
3. **Seek**: Deliberately seek God through His Word and prayer. Ask Him to reveal Himself to you fresh and new. (He loves this kind of request!)
4. **Listen**: Spend time in silence, allowing God to speak to your heart. Sometimes, reconnection starts with listening rather than speaking.
5. **Act**: Act on what God reveals to you. Obedience is a powerful form of worship and reconnection.

6. **Thank**: Always return to gratitude. Thank God for His unfailing love and for the grace that makes reconnection possible.

Take the above and write it on a 3x5 card or in a note-taking app on your phone. Look at it every morning and just dive in.

As we move forward, let these foundational practices and the pathway to reconnection guide our exploration of the victorious Christian life.

This journey is not about perfection but about growing ever closer to the One who has called us to victory in Him.

Now, drum roll...

It's time for VICTOROLOGY!

CHAPTER 1
THE EXCHANGED LIFE: THE ESSENTIAL KEY TO LIVE A VICTORIOUS LIFE

"When Christ calls a man, he bids him come and die."
— Dietrich Bonhoeffer

You know how at the beginning of a new year, you look back on the last one? You see what you did, what you didn't do; you see the mistakes you made and perhaps things you would like to change, but—if you're looking—you also see God's faithfulness. You got through it. God was good to you in ways you didn't understand, and He is going to show his faithfulness again.

I hope you're looking at the year in front of you with faith and excitement for what God's going to do because whether you're in the valley or on the mountaintop this year, God is still God. No matter how great last year was or how challenging it was, God was faithful, even when we were not, and I believe that He's going to do some things this year that are really going to build your faith.

I want to deliver some truths to you that I believe will be pivotal to your life this year—maybe even for the rest of your life. I want to take you on a journey in the Word of God to discover some transformational, fundamental, foundational truths that will make you ready for whatever comes your way, whether it's a bountiful blessing or a long, dark trial.

You've probably heard this: If you keep doing what you've always done, you'll get what you've always got. So true. As a matter of fact, some say "insanity" is doing what you've always done expecting different results.

In other words, if you do what you've always done but expect different results from doing those things, you're not "playing with a full deck," you're not "rowing with both oars," "the light isn't on in the attic," "the wheel is turning but the hamster is dead!"

Yet maybe that is exactly what describes your spiritual life. Maybe it describes most of your life for that matter.

With that in mind, I want to give you four things about the Christian life that I believe are transformational truths. Now, it's going to feel like I'm just giving you information, but how many of you know that sometimes there are certain types of information that are designed to lead to transformation? Sometimes you get certain information that you know is going to change your life— "You just won the lottery," "Your spouse did not make it through surgery," "Your mother-in-law is staying for the summer." I'm talking about information that says your life's about to change. So, as you read this chapter, I hope that you understand it's for the purpose of life transformation.

FOUR TRUTHS YOU CAN'T AFFORD TO IGNORE

Let's take a look at Galatians 2:17-20:

> But if, while we seek to be justified by Christ, we ourselves also are found sinners, is Christ therefore a minister of sin? Certainly not! For if I build again those things which I destroyed, I make myself a transgressor. For I through the law died to the law that I might live to

God. **I have been crucified with Christ; it is no longer I who live, but Christ lives in me; and the life which I now live in the flesh I live by faith in the Son of God, who loved me and gave Himself for me.**

In verses 17-19, Paul is quoting himself, literally what he said to Peter when he confronted Peter about his duplicity with the Jews and Gentiles and who he decided to eat with. He's talking about the law of Moses here when he says, "through the law I died to the law," but here's the point: "so that I might live to God." Now, we need to pray as we read these scriptures that the Holy Spirit of God, the Author, would unfold truth to our heart in a way that we would never ever be the same.

Have you ever noticed that if the tires on your car are wearing out too soon, mechanics usually say that they're out of balance or out of alignment? Something is wrong. Maybe you're like that. You are wearing yourself out, feeling the Christian life requires more effort than you could ever give it. What this means is, something in your life (or really, you're thinking) is out of alignment with one or more of these four truths.

These four transformational truths I'm about to give you about the Christian life are alignment truths. You're going to struggle in your walk with Christ to the degree that you do not believe and receive these four truths as being foundational to the Christian life. I would even go so far as to say that any struggle that you have in your life, any struggle you have in your marriage, any struggle you have in your attitude, any struggle you have with temptation, and any trouble you have in defeated areas of your life, can be traced back to not believing and receiving one of these four foundational truths about the Christian life.

These are four foundational truths that are absolutely true. They've always been true of the Christian life, and they will be true of the Christian life until Jesus comes. To the degree that we understand them and walk in them, we can live the overcoming, victorious, God-glorifying Christian life. What are those four truths? I'm going to give them to you.

FOUNDATIONAL TRUTH #1—THE CHRISTIAN LIFE IS A CRUCIFIED LIFE

In verse 20, Paul says, *"I have been crucified with Christ; it is no longer I who live, but Christ lives in me; and the life which I now live in the flesh I live by faith in the Son of God, who loved me and gave Himself for me."* He didn't get to the rest of verse 20 until he first laid down this pivotal truth: "I have been—say it with me—crucified with Christ." The Christian life is a "crucifix-ional" life. Why? Because in the same way that you and I could not be saved by keeping the law in our flesh, we cannot live the victorious, overcoming Christian life in our flesh. **In the same way that we got in the way of our own salvation, we get in the way of the victorious, overcoming Christian life.**

> *When God gave His people the law,*
> *He didn't give them the law to keep,*
> *He gave them the law to break.*

Let me ask you a question. Can you be saved by works? Can you be saved by keeping the law? When God gave His people the law, He didn't give them the law to keep, He gave them the law to break. He did not give them the law to keep. He gave them the law—613 Old Testament Mosaic laws, to be exact—but He didn't give them the law so that they could be saved by keeping it. Why? Because the way He was going to reveal that they were sinners in need of a Savior was by giving them a law that aligned with the holiness of God, a law that they could never fully keep themselves. So, the law functions not as a means of salvation but rather as a means to bring awareness of the need for salvation.

When I get out of bed in the morning and look at my face in

the mirror, the mirror will show me my face is dirty, but it will not wash my face. In the same way, the law shows us that we're law-breakers, but it provides no power in itself to help us keep the law or to help us earn salvation. So the first thing that happens when we come to Jesus is He reminds us that we are sinners. Now, you might be thinking what Paul says in verse 19: "Wait a minute, does that mean Christ is a minister of sin?" But Paul handles that question straightaway: "Certainly not. He's not a minister of sin." Listen, when somebody comes to Jesus, the first thing Jesus is going to point out to them is this: you're a sinner; you need a Savior, and I'm it. That's what Jesus is going to do.

But some people don't like to be told they're sinners. So what's the first default reaction? I'm going to go back to keeping the law. I'm going to cross all the t's and dot all the i's and be the best person I can be, and that'll save me. Here's what Paul says to that: "Through the law I became a transgressor. Through the law I died to the law." Literally, in the Greek, it means that I was dead, killed by the law. You can try to do good, try to do right, and try to save yourself. Then, on the other side of salvation, you can try to live for Jesus, but you will kill yourself trying—because you can't do it.

A fellow once went swimming with some friends. At some point, one of them got a leg cramp and began to drown. He was way out in the water when his leg froze up, so he tried to keep himself afloat. All the fellows' eyes went to the one among them who was a trained lifeguard and was sitting on the shoreline. But he didn't move. He sat in his chair staring at the drowning man, and they were left watching their friend flounder. They're wondering why he's not going to save him. Finally, when it seemed the friend had gone under for the last time, the lifeguard left his chair, dove into the water, dragged him to shore, and pumped the water from his lungs, saving his life.

The friends were mad and glad at the same time. They were

glad that the lifeguard saved the fellow's life but mad that he waited so long. When he was asked, "Why did you wait so long? We almost lost him."

He replied, "Because as long as a drowning man is exerting effort to save himself, not only will he not save himself, but his efforts will also inhibit the efforts of the one who is trying to save him. It is only when he entirely gives up that he can be saved at all." **Here's what's amazing: we got into this Christian life predicated on a confession that we could not save ourselves. Why on earth do we spend so much time on this side of salvation, thinking God needs our help to live the Christian life?**

The Christian life comes in three stages. In the first stage, *the Christian life is easy.* Do you remember that stage? Do you remember the day you got saved? Man, the day you got saved, the sun was shining, the birds were singing, and it was like all temptation had faded from the planet. You loved church, you loved all God's people, you loved the Bible, and you couldn't wait to read more and obey more. It was unbelievable. It was like, "This is great! I love living the Christian life. Why didn't I get saved sooner? The Christian life is easy."

That doesn't last too long, does it? Why? Because phase two kicks in eventually, and it's this: *The Christian life is difficult.* You begin to say, "Hey, wait a minute. It ain't easy living a Christian life. I'm going upstream in a downstream world. I'm wearing a white hat in a black hat world. The Christian life is tough. Living for Jesus is a challenge." The Christian life is difficult, but I want you to know that's only phase two of three. That is not where God wants you, and that's not where God is going to leave you because sooner or later, phase three has to kick in.

Phase one: the Christian life is easy. Phase two: the Christian life is difficult. Phase three: *the Christian life is impossible.* You can't live the Christian life by yourself, in your flesh, on your own.

You cannot do it, and if you try, you'll only get in the way. I'm telling you. I remember the day when I stretched myself across the bed in tears. I thought I'd checked all the boxes. I tried to please all the people I could please. I tried to do everything that I could do—the best ministry I could perform in my own flesh—and I exhausted myself as a very young man. And across the end of that bed, in tears, I looked up to God and meant it when I said, "That's it, God. I quit."

Now, I had always thought that if I ever looked at God and said, "I quit," all of a sudden, sirens would go off in heaven, angels would start running back and forth, and God would start popping Valium, thinking, "Oh no, what am I gonna do? Scott Smith quit." The day I looked up at God and said, "I quit," God looked back at me and said clearly, "Great. It's about time. **You've been getting in the way ever since I saved you.**"

The fact of the matter is we bring nothing to the table when we get saved. It is entirely dependent on the person of the Lord Jesus Christ and His work. And I'm telling you God has rigged the Christian life so that on this side of salvation, He is crucifying flesh and crucifying self so that we can finally live the Christian life as He gets us out of the way. Listen, you can take your best self to church. You can teach it manners. You can spiritualize it, sanitize it, and baptize it, but here's the truth: God don't want it. God's got one program for our best effort. God's got one program for self and flesh, and that program is a cross—"crucified with Christ."

> *"God's got one program for self and flesh, and that program is a cross—'crucified with Christ.'"*

This is Paul talking here—not gutter-crawling-drunk Paul; not addicted-to-pornography Paul; not cussing-filthy-mouthed Paul; this is Paul the Apostle. As a matter of fact, he was never any of those other things. He says, "I was a Jew among Jews. I was a Pharisee among Pharisees. I was born in the right tribe on the right day. I had the pedigree. I was trained by the best of the best." Listen, Paul was never a porn-addicted, gutter-crawling, drunk, brawling gossip. He was not any of those things. And yet, the Word of God is clear—even that Paul is on a crucifixion program, as he says, "I have been crucified."

Listen, we see this all throughout scripture, but we're so focused on salvation that we can miss it. Hear me, though. There is nothing wrong with salvation. We need to be focused on that. As a matter of fact, if you're reading this today, and you're not saved, you're not on your way to heaven, and you don't know Jesus, I hope you'll settle that before you stop reading. But if we stay there, we never learn how to get to victory, and Jesus has supplied everything we need for salvation and victory through His cross and resurrection.

He tried to remind us of it by starting things like communion and the Lord's Supper. There are two elements involved in the Lord's Supper, right? First of all, there's the wine (though in the Baptist Church, it's grape juice even though we serve it in a shot glass), and we know what it symbolizes regardless of what the substance is. It symbolizes the blood—the blood of Jesus Christ shed for the forgiveness of sins.

Then there's the other part of communion, which is what? The bread, or perhaps more commonly, the cracker. Maybe it shouldn't be called the Lord's Supper? The way we do it, maybe it ought to be called the Lord's Snack. All right, so we say the bread symbolizes the body, and we are now looking at the blood and the body. The blood symbolizes the removal of the penalty of sin, and Jesus then holds up on an almost equal plane the breaking of his body. If you pull a Baptist move and say "What does the breaking of the body symbolize?" they say, "I don't know." We don't know? But they're equally important.

One is about getting us into salvation. The other is about getting us into the overcoming Christian life. See, the body symbolizes the removal of the penalty of sin, but the breaking of the body symbolizes the breaking of the flesh, the removal of the power of sin in your life. One exists to defeat the penalty of sin, and the other exists to defeat the power of sin. **The blood symbolizes God taking us out of Adam (and putting us in Christ). The body broken symbolizes God taking the Adam out of us.** It is a crucifixion of life.

Now think about this: think about sin in your life. How do you deal with sin in your life? Our focus can typically be to suppress the sin. We have New Year's resolutions about suppressing the sin. We have accountability partners about suppressing the sin. We journal about how we're suppressing our sin. We're trying to attend another class on 12 steps to suppressing our sin. Our *modus operandi* is to suppress our sin, but God doesn't want us to suppress our sin. God wants us to let Him deal with the sinner. It's one thing to deal with the sin, but it's another thing entirely to deal with the sinner. It's one thing to crucify the sin, but God is trying to crucify the sinner.

In other words, God wants to remove the sinner through crucifixion so He can replace the sinner—and that's truth number two. It is an incarnation of life.

FOUNDATIONAL TRUTH #2—THE CHRISTIAN LIFE IS AN INCARNATION OF NEW LIFE

The Christian life according to Galatians 2:20 is not only a crucifixion of life but also an incarnation of life. Paul says, *"it is no longer I who live, but Christ lives in me."* Now, I want you to think about that. Christ lives in me. If you're saved by grace, if you're born again of the Spirit of God, if there's ever been a time in your life when you gave your heart to Jesus and the Spirit of

17

God came to dwell inside of you, then listen to me: Jesus lives inside of you.

Is that not amazing? Do you know who I'm talking about? I'm talking about the same Jesus who walked on water. I'm talking about the same Jesus who healed the blind man's eyes. I'm talking about the same Jesus who fed 5,000 people with the boy's fish and chips. I'm talking about the same Jesus who called Lazarus out of the four-day grave and got up out of His own grave after three days. I'm talking about Jesus living inside of you. Wow! Jesus lives inside of us!

All I just said is true, but there are two points of clarification needed: number one is that I'm not Christ—in the Bible, it's clear about that. I'm not Jesus, and He's not me. Number two is that my sins and my un-crucified flesh mark the margin of difference between who I function as right now and the unadulterated, uncompromised, personal potential of Christ in my life. That's why God has you on a crucifixion program, and if there's anything He's going to do this year, it's this: He's going to do as a good carpenter does, which is whatever it takes to sand down the rough edges of your flesh and self so that He can live more of His life through you.

The Christian life is not about going out and doing something great for God. The Christian life is about letting a great God live His life through you. It's not about us doing for Him. It's about Him doing in us. Why? Because the power of God dwells in us. It is incarnational.

> *The Christian life is about letting a*
> *great God live His life through you.*

Scientists tell us that if we were to replace the power of gravity—the invisible power that holds the earth suspended from the Sun and keeps it from floating off into outer space—with a steel rod, then that rod would have to be 25,000 miles in diameter to keep the Earth suspended from the Sun. But we don't have a rod of steel 25,000 miles in diameter; we have gravity. Through gravity, a bird can fly with ease. Through gravity, the song of that bird can be heard up to five miles away, depending on the species. And it's effortless despite that strong force called gravity.

Scientists still cannot explain that fully. I wish they could all hear me. I'm about to explain it for good. God. That's it. It's the power of God! It's the power of God at work all the time. We take it for granted but don't forget it. The Bible says that "in Him, we live and move and have our very being" (Acts 17:28). It is by Him that all things hold together. If He stopped doing whatever it is He's doing right now, we wouldn't even have gravity. We wouldn't be sitting here molecularly aligned at all if He did not display His power all the time. So understand that the power of God in Jesus dwells inside of you.

Let me explain it this way. What does the Bible say that God's standard is? The Bible says in Romans 3:23 that *"all have sinned and fallen short of the glory of God."* Sin means "to miss the mark." So here's God's standard: all have sinned and fall short of the glory of God. Now, let me give you another verse that talks about it, but in a different way and n a more obscure passage, Colossians 1:27. Listen to this: *"Christ in you is the hope of glory."* So all have sinned and fallen short of the glory of God, but somehow Christ in you is the hope of glory? Are you tracking with me?

Let me illustrate it this way. What if God said you had to golf a perfect par in order to go to heaven? Honey, don't even crank up the golf cart. I don't even have the skills to putt-putt well, alright? So what if God did say you had to golf par in order to go to heaven? You'd say, "Man, I'm sunk; it's over. Forget it." But what if there was a way to get Tiger Woods into my body? ZAP! Tiger Woods in me! All of a sudden, guess what? Now there's hope of golfing par. Right? See, Scott is not a good golfer, so I couldn't do that, but could Tiger Woods do it? Yes. As a matter of fact, he's done it over and over and over again.

Listen to me here. **All have sinned and fallen short of the glory of God, but the only hope for glory is this: it's Christ in me.** I can't do it, but Jesus can do it. I can't love them, but Jesus can love them. I can't raise my kids right, but Jesus can raise my kids right. I can't love my wife right, but Jesus can love my wife right. I can't forgive those who have hurt me, but Jesus can forgive those who have hurt me. I'm telling you, you can't live the Christian life, but Jesus can and wants to live it through you. Amen? Christ lives in me!

✦✦✦✦✦✦✦✦✦✦✦✦✦✦✦✦✦✦✦✦✦

PRAYING IT OUT

Father, I couldn't save myself, and now I can't help myself. I want to get out of the way. I'm tired of year after year trying to see what I can do, trying to perform better than I did last year. I realize that You've already condemned my performance, issuing the program of a cross on my life so that Your uncompromised, unfettered, unmitigated life, power, strength, and glory can live through me.

Good, bad, and ugly, come hell or high water, I want Jesus to dominate my life this year: His love, His life, His self-control, His fruit, His faithfulness. In the same way that I got saved, sure that there was nothing I could do to save me, I come to You on this side of salvation, certain that I've got nothing good to bring except You and what You do through me. In Jesus' Name, I pray. Amen.

LIVING IT OUT

As you try to receive the truth that the Christian life is a crucified life, you will run into real parts of yourself that just won't seem to go away. Try to think of some areas of your life that you have struggled to "put to death" for quite some time, and ask God what is standing in the way. What about God are you not trusting? When you struggle, do you lay hold of scriptural promises like Galatians 2:20 so that you can believe it? How can this truth about Christ crucifying your flesh and incarnating new life in you make a difference in your day to day walk of faith? This week, memorize Galatians 2:20, write it on your phone as a reminder, on your bathroom mirror, or wherever it is helpful, and tell yourself that reality whenever the old man rears its ugly head. Sooner or later, new life will begin to become manifest in you.

CHAPTER 2
THE EXCHANGED LIFE: CHRIST IN ME

*"The Christian life, from start to finish, is based
upon this principle of utter dependence upon the
Lord Jesus. There is no limit to the grace God is
willing to bestow on us. He will give us everything,
but only on the condition that we live for Christ."*
– Watchman Nee

We've been considering Paul's call to us to live crucified lives,
but as we face putting that old man to death, we recognize in
our soul the deep need to *replace* what we've lost. Or, to be more
accurate, as we allow God Himself to put that old man to death,
we'll see that He intends to put something (or someone) else in
its place. In other words, God wants to *remove* the sinner so He
can *replace* the sinner.

Think about how you deal with sin in your life. You focus on
suppressing the sin. But God focuses on *removing* the sinner. We
focus on destroying the *product*. God focuses on destroying the
factory. Why? So He can put something in its place that produces
an entirely different product!

To the degree that the Christian life is a "crucifixional" life, it
is also an "incarnational" life! God's promise is clear: an incarnation of new life only comes through the resurrection—Christ
in us, the hope of glory.

Now, here is the question you might have: How do you tap into that incarnational power of that new Christ life in us? Well, Paul gives us an answer right there in Galatians 2:20. He says, "the life I now live, I live by faith." By faith! When I really started seeing that, I was shocked. I grew up in church, but I was still amazed when I saw how central faith was, how it's the key to living the Christian life.

Actually, the Bible speaks about faith pretty radically when it comes to its importance and centrality to an effective Christian life.

Consider these verses.

Galatians 3:11: *"The righteous shall live by faith."* So there is no hope for Scott Newton Smith living righteously apart from faith.

How about this one:

Hebrews 11:6: "Without faith it is highly unlikely you'll please God." No, that's not what it says. *"Without faith it is **impossible** to please God."* He didn't say "highly unlikely." He said, "impossible!"

Or, this one:

Romans 14:23: *"Anything that does not come from faith is sin."* What does "anything" mean? "Anything" means "everything." "Everything" means "anything." *Anything* that does not take off from the launching pad of faith is *counted as sin*. What does anything cover again? Anything covers everything. Anything even means *things attempted for God*. (Oof!)

Let's look at an example. Let's say that today two men are taking a pulpit on opposite ends of town. One guy is standing up to preach a sermon he's preached a thousand times in his life. He knows it by heart, doesn't use his notes, and every illustration and exegetical principle is right. When he gives that invitation, every time he sees people get saved. Every time. Now today he's going to preach this sermon the 1001st time.

"God doesn't want to see what you can do for Him. God wants to see what you can let Him do through you."

Across town there's another fellow preaching. Let's say he's going to preach the first sermon he's ever preached in his life. His pastor was going out of town for the holidays and asked him to preach, but the guy said, "I've never preached before," and the pastor just replied, "do what you can." So the guy is preaching in front of his church the first sermon he's ever preached in his life. Now we have one guy who's got all the experience and all the feedback, then we have a guy who's never preached before, and they're both stepping up to preach at the same time in two different churches on opposite sides of town.

Here's the question. Which one needs the most faith? The true answer is *both*. Both need the same faith as much as they can leverage. Both need to approach the pulpit hopelessly, helplessly dependent on the working of the Word and the Spirit of God saying, "I've got nothing to bring except the only good thing in me, and that is Jesus Himself. And God, if it doesn't happen by your hand, it's going to be worth nothing." God doesn't want to see what you can do for Him. God wants to see what you can let Him do through you. That's faith.

Jesus said "apart from Me you can do nothing," not "some things," not "a few things." Wait a minute. Did Jesus really say that apart from Him you can do *nothing*?

You may say, "Well, I drive a car without Him. I can brush my teeth without Him. I can raise money without Him. I can print books without Him. I could go work a job without Him. Goodness, just look at all the people who don't even know Him who get massive wealth and fame, and they don't even know Him!"

What did Jesus mean by "apart from me you can do nothing?"

Jesus meant that **even what you can do apart from Him amounts to nothing apart from Him.**

The truth is that both of the men in the preaching illustration need the same amount of faith, all the faith that God will give them. Why? Because it's the guy who's never preached before who's probably going to lean on Jesus the most. I'm telling you, the guy who's preached a thousand times may be effective, he may be anointed, he may be good, but understand that it is he who has the greatest temptation not to rely on God as he should. **That is why our greatest strength can often become our greatest weakness to the degree that it displaces helpless dependence on the power of God.** Remember, the Christian life is an incarnation of life. It is a crucifixional life. It is also a devotional life.

FOUNDATIONAL TRUTH #3—THE CHRISTIAN LIFE IS A DEVOTIONAL LIFE

Paul said, "I live by faith in the Son of God who loved me." Hey, every hour, tell yourself this truth: Jesus loves you. You say "Man, you don't know how I blew it." Jesus loves you. "Scott, I've been out of fellowship and away from God so long." Jesus loves you. "But you have no idea, I shook my fist at God!" Jesus loves you.

Now, why is it important that we understand the Christian life is a devotional life? Because **to the degree that I do not believe that He loves me and that His love is enough, I will manipulate and milk people to feed the need for love in my life.** And in so doing, I will mess up my ministry; I'll mess up my marriage; I'll mess up my parenting, and I'll mess up my testimony because I'll see people as objects that exist to give me what I think I need the most. I will use them to get the love I crave in my heart because their love is the only love I think I can get. But I'm telling you, there is no greater or more freeing truth than to know that what people say about me doesn't matter. It doesn't matter what people think of me. It doesn't matter if people lie about me. What matters is what God thinks, what He knows. He loves me. He accepts me, and that is enough for me. I'm free! Amen.

> *"When we believe fully that God's love is enough, we're free to love and serve others with no strings attached."*

Listen, when we believe fully that His love is enough, we're free to bless people, we're free to minister to people, we're free to serve people—listen to me here—*with no strings attached*. Thank God that the Christian life is a devotional life. Why? Because we are a people desperately in need of love, and He is a God who desperately wants to offer His love. So why don't we get together and just make it alright? This is the devotional life. But it's also a substitutional life, as Paul says of Jesus that He was the one "who loved me and *gave Himself* for me."

FOUNDATIONAL TRUTH #4—THE CHRISTIAN LIFE IS A SUBSTITUTIONAL LIFE

We believe in the church that the Bible teaches something called substitutional atonement. That means my sins were deserving of punishment, but Jesus died on the cross in my place and for my sins. So what did that do? That made sure that 100% of the wrath of God that was stored up as just punishment for my sins was poured out on Jesus instead on the cross 2,000 years ago. So when the Devil says, "Scott is deserving of death for his sins," that is true. But God says, "No, he's already died for his sins. His sins have already been punished by death." When did that happen? It happened 2,000 years ago on a rugged cross. That is substitutional atonement.

So when we say "Jesus died for me," here's what we're really saying: He died *as* me.

And guess what? He didn't just die for me. He was buried for me. It was a substitutional burial in the same way that it was a substitutional crucifixion. So when He died as me, *He was also buried as me*. The Bible says that God united us with Christ in His death, and He united us with Christ in His burial. "We were buried with Him," Roman 6 tells us. Did it stop there? No, it did not, because—three days later—up from the grave He arose. And guess what? When He came out, you came out. We're a brand-new creation in the Lord Jesus Christ! We have been united with Him in His resurrection because when He was raised for me, he was raised *as* me.

But it didn't stop there either. Just 40 days later, He ascended to heaven. Do you know that He ascended substitutionally, just like He died substitutionally, was buried substitutionally, and was raised substitutionally? You ascended with Christ when He ascended. That is why Colossians 3:2-3 can tell us to *"Set your mind on things above, not on things on the earth. For you died, and your life is hidden with Christ in God."* Jesus died for me. He died as me. He was buried as me. He was raised as me. He ascended as me. So if you're asking me if I'm going to heaven when I die, you're wasting your time, because I'm already there.

Now do I fully understand that? No, but I don't understand airplane cockpits or aeronautics either. I don't need enough faith to fly the thing. I just need enough faith to get myself into the seat so the pilot who knows it all can get me to the destination. And that's what you need in the Christian life. Faith. He'll take you there by faith, because of His substitutional life.

By the way, we are His substitute on the earth, as much as He was for us on Calvary. Let's be honest, if He'd have been only as committed to us as we are to Him, He'd never have gone to the cross.

So let's ask God to work in us. Lord, let me be Your hands; let me be Your feet; let me be Your voice; let me be Your life; let me be Your message to this generation. It is a substitutional life.

It's a crucifixional life.

It's an incarnational life.

It's a devotional life.

It's a substitutional life.

These are alignment truths. You and I will struggle to have an overcoming life to the degree that you and I are not fully embracing these truths.

COMING INTO ALIGNMENT: THE GLOVE AND THE BOOK ILLUSTRATION

Now, what does all this look like in life?

Picture a table. Now picture a dirty white glove laying on that table. Now imagine beside the glove is a thick, hardback book.

Now, with that picture in your mind, I'm going to ask you a question in a moment, and I want you to give me an answer. The answer has to be yes or no. You have to commit to an answer. There is no right or wrong, just commit to an answer. And here's the question: Can the glove pick up the book? Some people will wholeheartedly say yes, and others will say absolutely not.

I figure that the truth is simple: no, it can't pick up the book. It can't pick up the book, because I didn't tell it to. So excuse me a second while I speak to the glove. "Okay, glove, it's time. Pick up the book." Is that going to happen? No. Do you know that you and I cannot live the Christian life as an overcomer by being told to live the overcoming Christian life any more than the glove can pick up the book by being told to do it? Yet today, 90% of what we do in church is oriented around telling people to go live for Jesus. And we wonder why they can't do it.

Okay, I see the problem. The glove can't lift the book, because I didn't tell it how. Silly me. "Okay glove, you're going to lift the book. Here's how you're gonna lift it. You're pretty flat, so you're going to take a running start, and you're going to slide those four fingers underneath, throw the thumb over the top, press with equal pressure, and lift the book. Now do it." This isn't working. Now, did I tell it how to? Was I right in what I told it? Yes.

Yet, thousands of books are flying off of Christian bookstore shelves left and right, year-in and year-out, telling Christians *how* to live for Jesus, *how* to live the overcoming life, but most people sitting in most pews in most churches in America won't do it even one week after reading one of those books or attending church on a Sunday. I'm telling you why. It's because you and I can't live the overcoming Christian life by being told *how* any more than that glove can lift that book by being told *how* to do it.

Oh, I see the problem. The problem is that the glove has no motivation. So excuse me while I motivate my glove with a little action anthem: "Rah-rah-sis-boom-bah, you're a glove, and you can pick up the book. If you believe it, you can do it!"

Is that going to work? No. But think about it. How many times have we taught like that, preached like that, led like that, parented like that? We've even told ourselves, as we're sitting down writing resolutions at the beginning of a new year, "Man, if I can just get enough motivation. Man, if we can just feel it enough, then baby, we're going to do it this time!" I'm telling you, emotions are the most fickle part of who we are. You have a mind, you have a will, and you have emotions. **God wants to be involved in your emotions, but He is primarily after your mind and your will.** Yet, we judge 90% of what happens in church by how it makes us feel. We will meet the pastor at the back door of the church and say, "Boy, Pastor, the Lord sure was in there today, like I haven't felt Him in a long time." (Last time I checked, where two or more are gathered, He's there—whether you feel it or not.) We measure the work of God by our emotions and too often conclude that God's work in us resided there primarily. Here's the takeaway: *we must not expect God to do His deepest work in our shallowest part.*

There's nothing wrong with emotions; don't get me wrong. But emotions change quickly and, as a motivator, emotions fade quickly. In light of that, I sure am glad my salvation is based on faith and not feeling. It's not about how you and I feel.

> *"If you rely on your feelings, all it takes to convince you God isn't working in your life is a bit of bad pizza."*

Alright, alright, so I know that glove's problem now. That glove has no discipline. That's why he can't pick up that book. Look at him. Floppy, lazy-looking glove. There's not enough force being exerted on the inside of him to keep him from conforming to whatever he is around on the outside. (Do you know any Christians like that?) So what this glove needs is discipline. So let's give him a good talking to: "You stupid glove, if you were worth anything, you'd pick up that book. Do it, or you're just a good-for-nothing glove." Is the glove going to pick up that book now? Still, the answer is no.

Yet, how many churches are largely built on the notion that if we can just make people feel bad enough and guilty enough, they'll finally be moved to get out there and live for God? Man, you can go into churches sometimes that are packed to the gills, and some preacher will get up there and be ripping into you talking about what a dirty, rotten scoundrel you are and telling you how hell will be glad to have you, because heaven doesn't want you. He'll be telling you how you haven't been living for God, how you're little more than the sum of all that's wrong with you, and how you ought to be ashamed of yourself, and so on. Sometimes I hear those guys and I'm thinking, "Man, what in the world happened to that preacher? Was he just sitting in a study all week saying 'Hmm, how can I cuss them out on Sunday morning in the name of Jesus? How can I let them have it? I ain't preaching good until I've cut their head clean off at the shoulders and they're walking out thanking God for it.'"

You've been in some of those churches, and people are glad to go to them, and here's why: "I've been doing a lot of bad stuff this week, and I feel really guilty. I feel so guilty and so bad that I'm going to go down to the church, and my pastor is going to spank me real good. I like getting a good beating because it makes my conscience feel better. I know by the end of the service he's going to beat me up so good, I can go out again and do the same thing next week knowing next Sunday's coming."

This is how they congratulate the pastor on a good job: "Thank you, Pastor, you really stepped on my toes." Listen, I know what's meant by that. I've said that myself. And certainly, there is a place for rebuke in the church, don't misunderstand. But do understand this, all you're experiencing is guilt in ministries that are built on inducing it as a transformational tool. And do you know how you deal with guilt as a born-again child of God? You don't have to go to a priest. You don't have to go to a preacher. He doesn't stand between you and God. We go straight to the throne. We boldly approach the throne of grace to find help in our time of need (Hebrews 4:16). You need to understand that the reason God hears my confession prayer is not that I did all the right things this week, it's because the blood of Jesus is available to me daily to cleanse me from my sin.

Guilt is a lousy motivator, and it certainly doesn't transform. It won't help a Christian live an overcomer's life any more than it will move that glove to lift that book.

All right, so I'm finally sure about the problem with this glove: it's dirty. It's disqualified for service. So I need to send it home to get washed. Let's say I go wash it, bring it back here, and lay it next to the book, clean. Now the disqualification has been removed. So let's see it lift the book. Is the glove going to do it?

No. Why?

Just because the disqualification has been removed doesn't mean there is anything inserting power to do what it needs to do. If the best you're offering God is the fact that you've been forgiven and your sins have been removed, you're not getting into the overcoming Christian life. You're basically offering God a blank. I found that most Christians offer God either a blank or a blot, and God wants to make you a blessing.

Something else has to happen. So what's the answer? Here's the answer, and it's found in Galatians chapter four, verse nineteen.

TAKING SHAPE

Galatians 4:19 reads: *"My little children, for whom I labor in birth again until Christ is formed in you..."*

Now, did Paul mean they were his biological kids? No. He meant he was their spiritual father. He had brought them to Jesus. He had birthed them into God. They are his spiritual offspring.

Look at what he says, "my little children for whom I labor in birth *again*." "Again" means *twice*. The first time, he labored to birth them into salvation. Now, he's laboring to get them into the overcoming Christian life. The first time was to get them into Jesus. The second time was to get them to walk in victory through Jesus.

Let's keep going—He says he labors in birth until "Christ is formed in you."

Now, you need to understand there are two Greek words that can be translated into English as "formed." One is the word *schema*, which means "outward formation." If I get a lump of clay, and I mash it and poke it, I'm *schema-ing* it. I'm forming it. That is *not* the word Paul used here in Galatians 4:19 that is translated "formed." The other Greek word that is often translated as "formed" is the one he uses here. It is the word *morphe*. It does not indicate an outward change. It means inward change. It doesn't mean outward power is being applied to shape an object, it means inner power is being applied to transform it. What it really means here is *there's a power that is so forceful and dynamic on the inside that it breaks into visibility on the outside.*

Now, if earlier in the chapter, you answered the glove-and-book question with, "Yes, the glove can pick up the book," what were you thinking? You were thinking it would work, if...what? *If you put your hand in it.* The glove can pick up the book only if you put your hand in it. But you know what a lot of people do? They do what is the equivalent of placing their hand inside the glove in the form of a fist. Now imagine that. You said, "Place your hand inside the glove and it can then pick up the book." Your suggestion is accurate—but not adequate. All that is the hand—by definition—is inside the glove—but all balled up. Then the glove, with the hand inside, moves to the book to lift it. But the fingers of the glove are still empty. It can only brush the floppy fingers against the book, powerless to do any lifting. The glove is exhausted and the book remains unmoved.

So many of us are like that. A lot of people say, "Well, now I've arrived. I'm ready to go. I've got Jesus in my heart. I've got Jesus in my life." But here's the truth: for year, after year, after year—in the face of trials, temptations, challenges, storms, and blessings— you wonder why you're not living the overcoming Christian life, even though Jesus is inside of you. And here's the problem. He's still just knotted up on the inside. Then you apply more "glove power" to your situations, forgetting the glove doesn't have any power. And Jesus is still knotted up on the inside.

When God says He's to be fully formed in you, He's talking about an inward change so powerful and forceful on the inside that it breaks into visibility on the outside. This is how you're going to do whatever God says He wants you to do. This is how you're going to be able to say whatever God says He wants you to say. This is how you're going to be able to resist whatever God mandates you resist. This is how you're going to accomplish whatever God says He wants to accomplish this year. This is how you're going to live the overcoming Christian life. You're going to do it with Jesus fully extended throughout every finger of the glove.

I don't know what your "book" is. But I know there is a "book" waiting to be lifted. God is calling us to something great, calling us to something bigger than ourselves. God is calling us to do something significant, and the only way we're going to undertake any divine calling—no matter how big or small—is if Jesus is fully formed in us.

Understand, the glove has no power in and of itself. It can do its best, and as much "effort" as it applies it will never be enough. **However, the glove can do whatever the hand can do as long as it's cooperating with, submitted to, and surrendered under that hand.**

> *"Whatever God calls you to do, you can do, as long as He does it through you."*

The Christian life is not about straining, it's about containing. The Christian life is not about trying, it's about trusting. This Christian life is not about morality, it's about spirituality. The Christian life is not flesh-based, it is faith-based. You will wear yourself out trying to live it on your own strength.

I'm telling you, whatever God calls you to do, you can do, as long as He does it through you. Jesus doesn't want to *give* you peace. He *is* your peace. He doesn't want to *give* you joy. He *is* your joy. He doesn't want to *give* you strength. He is your strength. He doesn't want to *give* you life. He *is* your life. Letting Jesus be Jesus in you is the key to the Christian life.

PRAYING IT OUT

Father, I love You today. I pray in the name of Jesus that You would find me surrendered, yielded, hungry, eager—desperate even—for Your life and power. Make the difference in my marriage. Make the difference in my finances. Make the difference in my body and my mind. Make the difference in my emotional health. Make the difference in my impact. Make the difference in my ministry. Lord, You are the difference. You're the only difference. I pray You make the difference today in me, in Jesus' name.

LIVING IT OUT

How often do you do things for God? What's the last thing you did for Him lately? How'd you feel afterwards? Now, take those thoughts and face them with this reality: "God doesn't want to see what you can do for Him. God wants to see what you can let Him do through you." How does that change the way you are thinking about your recent track record of obedience? Many of us know the verse that says, *"I can do all things through Christ who strengthens me"* (Philippians 4:13).

Ask yourself whether you actually let Jesus live this life for you. Are the many things you are doing really being done by

Jesus empowering you through surrender? Are you that glove He can put His hand in and move around? Try to get before God this week and start a habit of laying your life down before Him, asking Him to decide what happens in a day, asking Him to use you as He sees fit. Then obey every time you get a chance so you can see the fruit that comes through it.

CHAPTER 3
THE OVERCOMER'S IDENTITY: WHO AM I?

*"Understanding your identity in Christ
is absolutely essential to your success at
living a victorious Christian life."*
– Neil T. Anderson

Once you understand that your life is not your own, that you were *"bought with a price"* (1 Cor. 6:20) and can say to yourself when you get up in the morning, *"It is no longer I who live but Christ who lives in me,"* (Gal. 2:20) then you can begin to really live the overcoming Christian life. To make this transition, though, it's not so much about *what you do* as it is about who you are because of what Jesus has done for you. Through His finished work, you are a new creation, and you're on a lifelong journey of discovering exactly what that means. To start, let's take a look at Romans chapter six.

As we look at this passage, we want to talk about overcoming patterns of defeat, specifically by leveraging your new identity in Jesus. When Jesus changes a life, he *really* changes a life. We're going to talk about how deep that actually goes because I believe that many times we believers really don't see that—we really don't understand it fully.

I know a lot of you are like me in that you grew up in church. You've heard all the sermons, sung all the songs, and read all the verses. But have you ever had that experience where you've read a verse a thousand times, and then on the thousand and first time, it just jumps off the page into your life? You're thinking, "Man, how have I never seen this? I've read it before but never noticed this!" And it was that one insight that changed everything for you.

I believe Romans chapter six is one of those passages. You and I both know that sometimes we can run through the scriptures a little carelessly. Many of us have started year-long Bible reading plans, and that is great. I have those people coming up to me all the time saying, "Brother Scott, I read my Bible cover to cover every single year."

I'm thinking, "That's all well and good, but you can run through a grocery store and still starve to death." The question is, when you read the Word of God, are you *interacting* with what's there? Are you going deep with the Word of God the Lord Himself has entrusted to you to study?

The process reminds me of one of Sherlock Holmes' adventures. On one occasion, the detective and his sidekick, Watson, were out on a camping trip. They were in their sleeping bags getting ready to sleep when Sherlock Holmes—always mentoring Watson—asked Watson a question. "Watson, look up and tell me what you see."

So Watson looked up and replied, "I see a sky full of stars."

Sherlock continued, "Okay, and what do you deduce from that? What conclusion do you draw from that observation?"

Wanting to impress Sherlock, Watson said, "Well, astrologically, it tells me there are millions upon millions of stars, perhaps thousands upon thousands of galaxies in our universe. Meteorologically, it tells me we're in for good weather tomorrow. Theologically, it tells me God is amazing in what He can create with the spoken word. What does it tell you, Sherlock?"

Sherlock's reply was quick: "Well, it tells *me* that somebody stole our tent."

Now, Watson sounds like a fool here, but let's just admit it—sometimes, you're looking right at something profoundly important, and you just don't see it. And I believe that Romans 6 is one of *those* sorts of passages.

So, how do you break the cycles of defeat we face day in and day out while trying to live the Christian life? This is exactly the question Paul is answering. Let's go to verse one together. This will start a little slow at first because I want to lay some foundations, then it will pick up speed. Here we go.

HOW TO BREAK CYCLES OF DEFEAT

Romans 6:1-4

> What shall we say then? Shall we continue in sin that grace may abound? Certainly not! How shall we who died to sin live any longer in it? Or do you not know that as many of us as were baptized into Christ Jesus were baptized into His death? Therefore we were buried with Him through baptism into death, that just as Christ was raised from the dead by the glory of the Father, even so we also should walk in newness of life.

Let's stop right at verse one. *"What shall we say then? Shall we continue in sin that grace may abound?"* All of us know what it's like on this side of salvation. If you're saved—if you're born again—you've given your life to Jesus, and you're seeing that when you sin now, what happens? Well, you feel bad about it, don't you? As a matter of fact, if you think you're saved and don't feel bad when you're saying something wrong, you had better check out your salvation. Can I get an "Amen?"

So you feel bad, and if you handle it biblically, you're going to confess your sin when you feel guilty, and you're going to get it right with God and be cleansed and restored in relationship with Him. That's awesome. And you're going to move on. But how many of us also know what it's like—after some time passes, maybe an hour, maybe a day, maybe a week, maybe a few weeks—to sin again? Now, I don't mean just any sin, but *that* sin, the same one that tripped you up the first time around that you swore you never wanted any part of again. So what happens when you feel bad again? And when you feel guilty again and confess it again? And then a little more time passes, and you sin *again* that same sin.

Then what? I'm talking about that sin or set of sins that seem to be leftovers from the old life rooted in your flesh that won't shift no matter how hard you try. Don't you know this cycle? You sin, feel guilty, confess; sin, feel guilty, confess; sin, feel guilty, confess. See the pattern? You begin to develop a pattern of defeat in some area (or several areas) in your life.

Here's what I've found in my own life and in the lives of *so many* believers I've counseled. It's this: if that cycle repeats itself long enough without changing, and we can't seem to get victory over that area of repeated defeat, that continual sin cycle, then *we tend to begin making excuses for the pattern.* We begin to say things like:

"Well, you know, all the men in my family struggled with this."

"Well, you know, nobody's perfect."

"Well, you know, we're not in heaven yet."

"Well, you know, *everybody's* got a vice."

And on the list goes.

As we begin to make excuses, here's what happens in practical terms: we resign ourselves to defeat, and we assume that it's okay because we haven't been able to change it. "Well, at least I'm *saved*, after all, and thank God for that, but as far as *a life characterized by victory* goes, it just doesn't work for me."

But I'm telling you on the authority of the Word of God that *this ought not to be the case* for the child of God. In other words, **there's not a single area of your new life as a born-again child of God that He does not intend to inject with a full dose of victory.**

BELIEF DETERMINES BEHAVIOR

Paul writes to the heart of the problem: *"Shall we continue in sin that grace may abound?"* Verse two provides the clear answer: *"Certainly not!"* Read the next verses: *"How shall we who died to sin live any longer in it? Or do you not **know** that as many of us as were baptized into Christ Jesus were baptized into His death?"*

I want to stop right there for another observation. Notice this: Paul uses the word "know" regularly and strategically. Throughout the passage, in this verse and the ones to follow, Paul uses the word *"know"* or some similar Greek word that relates to the word "knowledge" at regular intervals. Why? Because he's dealing with repeated cycles of defeat, strongholds, and footholds that became strongholds. In order to deal with those, he understands that knowledge is key.

See, it's what you *know* that determines how you *go*. It is your beliefs that determine your behavior. You live like you live because you believe like you believe. Paul wants us to understand that **the reason we have a behavior problem is that we've got a belief problem**.

> *"What you know determines how you go. Your beliefs determine your behavior. An error in your living is a result of an error in your thinking."*

As a matter of fact, knowledge is *so* key that you'll find this every single time Paul writes a letter. You could take any letter Paul wrote and cut it down the middle, and here's what you'll notice: the first half of the letter is doctrinal in nature, and the second half is practical in nature. In the first half, he'll spend time telling you what to believe, and in the second half, he'll spend time telling you how to live. Now, why does Paul do it in that order and not the other way around? Because *he understands that he can't fix how you live if he hasn't first fixed what you believe.* An error in your living is a result of an error in your thinking.

Think about it. What did God say in Hosea 4:6? He said, "My people perish for lack of *knowledge.*" Jesus said, "...you will *know the truth*, and the truth will set you free" (John 8:32). In other words, there's no freedom to be found without knowing the truth.

By the way, that's why the Devil wants to keep you out of church. He wants to keep you away from the truth. Why? Because his agenda for you is *bondage.* Jesus' agenda for you is *freedom.* How does that freedom come? Through exposure to the truth. The formula won't ever change.

THE FORMULA FOR TRANSFORMED THINKING

You don't *naturally* think like Jesus thinks. You don't *naturally* see things like Jesus sees them. Why? Because *"'My thoughts are not your thoughts, nor are your ways My ways,' says the Lord. 'For as the heavens are higher than the earth, so are My ways higher than your ways, and My thoughts than your thoughts'"* (Isaiah 55:8-9). That's so true. I mean, really—Jesus is "backward" on most things when compared to man's default thinking. You have to give in order to receive, He says. You have to lose your life in order to find it, He says. You have to humble yourself in order to be exalted, He says. We don't think like that.

The world doesn't think like that. And even we Christians don't naturally think like that just by virtue of being born again. We've got to expose ourselves to truth regularly. You have to know the truth in order to be set free. There's freedom in being exposed to the truth. That's why the Devil wants to keep you away from the truth.

Have you ever noticed that if you want to play Xbox, you can have at it all day, and it's no problem? If you want to go out for a game of golf, that's just fine. When you want to watch a movie, work in your garden, or read a book, no big deal. But if you open your Bible, all of a sudden—doors are slamming, sirens are going off, dogs are barking, and babies are crying (and there aren't even any in the house!) Am I right? The Devil will do *whatever he can* to keep you out of that book. Why? Because he's got bondage in mind for you, and the truth—he knows it—will set you free, so he fights your exposure to God's Truth every step. *You* just have to know it, and you have to *commit* to going to get it.

What you know determines how you go; your beliefs determine your behavior. That's why Paul uses this word "know" in verse three:

> ... do you not **know** that as many of us as were baptized into Christ Jesus were baptized into His death? Therefore we were buried with Him through baptism into death, that just as Christ was raised from the dead by the glory of the Father, even so we also should walk in newness of life. For if we have been united together in the likeness of His death, certainly we also shall be in the likeness of His resurrection, knowing this, that our old man was crucified with Him, that the body of sin might be done away with, that we should no longer be slaves of sin (Romans 6:3-6).

Look at that last line again, and then continue through verse 14: "*...that we should no longer be slaves of sin.*" Why? Because

> ...he who has died has been freed from sin. Now, if we died with Christ, we believe that we shall also live with Him, knowing that Christ, having

been raised from the dead, dies no more. Death no longer has dominion over Him. For the death that He died, He died to sin once for all, but the life that He lives, He lives to God. Likewise, you also (Here comes another "knowing" word) **reckon** yourselves to be dead indeed to sin, but alive to God in Christ Jesus our Lord. Therefore do not let sin reign in your mortal body, that you should obey it in its lusts. And do not present your members as instruments of unrighteousness to sin, but present yourselves to God as being alive from the dead and your members as instruments of righteousness to God. For sin shall not have dominion over you, for you are not under law but under grace.

KNOWING WHO YOU ARE IN CHRIST

So, how do you break those strongholds? How do you walk out of those defeat cycles? How do you live this changed life? Whatever that sin is, it's mastering you, whether it's something you look at or something you say, whether it's your temper or the thoughts in your head; that thing runs your life, that thing you wish you could change that never seems to change. How do you get out of that trap? First of all, *you've got to know who you are in Christ.* I repeat: you have got to know and receive your new identity in Christ as a result of your new birth. In verse one of Romans six, he lays out the problem, and in verse two, he starts dealing with the problem and notice how he deals with it right off the bat. He first reminds them of their identity: *"Certainly not, how shall we who died to sin live any longer in it?"*

And who are we again, brother Paul? **We are those *"who died to sin."*** The first thing that he's doing here is reminding them of their new identity in Jesus, that they are a people who have (past tense) died to sin. Why? Because, as we have already observed, beliefs determine behavior. Because what you know determines how you go. Because identity is at the core of what is or is not being produced in your life.

46

One time, a man went to the doctor, and he said, "Doctor, listen, I've got big problems with my wife."

The doctor asked, "What kind of problems?"

The man continued, "Well, for the last four years, my wife has believed she's a chicken."

The doctor looked shocked. "Excuse me, what did you say?"

The man said, "She believes she's a chicken. She walks around the house all day pecking, squawking, doing the whole chicken thing."

The doctor decided to dig a little deeper, "What about the other part?"

The man looked confused. "What other part?"

The doctor gave him an inquisitive look. "You said four years. That's a long time!"

The man responded, "Yeah, the four longest years of my life."

The doctor concluded, "Well, my question for you is this: why didn't you come to me sooner?"

The man shrugged. "We really needed the eggs."

> *"Identity is at the core of what is or is not being produced in your life."*

What I'm saying is this: there are real things being produced in your life, the "eggs" that can be directly traced back to your sense of identity—who you see yourself to be. Now I'll turn the same coin. On the other side, there are things that are *not* being produced in your life that you know ought to be produced—spiritually, relationally, morally, whatever, that can also be traced back to who you see yourself to be. What's on the inside—your thoughts—gets fleshed out on the outside.

By the way, that's why you had better be careful who or what speaks into your thoughts. The Bible tells us in 2 Corinthians 10:5

to *take every thought captive in obedience to Jesus Christ.* That's why as a born again believer, I can't watch just any old kind of movie. I can't listen to just any old kind of music. I can't just let any old kind of philosophy get into my head. Why? Because what gets into the *mind* comes out into the *life* sooner or later. What does the Bible say? Proverbs 23:7 tells us, *"As a man thinks in his heart, so is he."* **What you think is what you are.** Have you ever heard that? What you think is what you are.

So, if our thinking about our identity is not aligned with the Word of God, we will not have the output in our lives that God intended. We'll have the opposite of that because whatever fills the mind fills the life.

As a matter of fact, the progression is always the same as noted often throughout history:

"Sow a thought and you reap an action; sow an act and you reap a habit; sow a habit and you reap a character; sow a character and you reap a destiny." —Ralph Waldo Emerson

"Spiritual strongholds begin with a thought. One thought becomes a consideration. A consideration develops into an attitude, which leads then to action. Action repeated becomes a habit, and a habit establishes a 'power base for the enemy,' that is, a stronghold." —Elisabeth Elliot

So that's why we have to get God's Truth into our mind, I mean really believe and accept it. And the primary Truth we need to begin with is the one about who we really are in Christ.

As Adrian Rogers once put it: "The Me I see is the Me I'll be!" (Hey, memorize that!)

But you need to be warned, *it might be one of the most difficult doctrines to fully embrace.*

Yep. That's right. I said it. I believe out of all the doctrines that we hear about—justification, sanctification, redemption—the one that we have the hardest time getting our minds around and really embracing as true for us is the one about our new identity in Jesus.

THE PLAGUE OF PERFORMANCE-BASED IDENTITY (AND ITS ORIGINS)

You might say, "Scott, why do you believe it's so hard for us to embrace who we really are in Jesus after we're saved?" I'll tell you why. It's because we are born into, raised up in, and surrounded by *a world system that defines identity along completely different lines than God defines it.*

For instance, the world says you are who you are based on:

- What you've performed in the past
- How you perform in the present
- The opinions of others about your performance (and your person)

The world is so strong with its messages about identity that this creeps even into the church and the thinking of so many Christians.

LIE OF THE WORLD #1: YOU ARE YOUR PAST PERFORMANCE

Let's take, for instance, the idea that identity is based on what we've done in the past. Let's say a guy has been in prison for 25 years because 25 years ago, he was tried and convicted for murder. We don't even know the whole story. Now, he's out of prison, on parole, and walking around in society. How do people talk about him?

There'll be two people talking. One will say, "Hey man, stay away from that guy."

"Why?" the other asks.

"Oh, you don't know?" The first person continues. "He's a murderer."

The second person seems concerned. "Well, when did he get convicted?"

If the first person is honest, finally, the truth comes out. "Oh, about 25 years ago."

Now, the fellow might have gotten saved in prison and even started the biggest Bible study that prison system has ever seen, but now he's walking around in the culture, and they're filling in the blanks on his identity based on what he did back then—regardless of what is true. They even speak in the present tense, "he *is* a..." That's the way the world works, *not God*.

Quite frankly, we do this to each other. And we do it to ourselves in our inner conversations.

That is one reason you can't seem to get past the sins of your past. You might have read a little about forgiveness. Perhaps you prayed and asked God to forgive you. Maybe you even gave your life to Jesus, and you really believed the preacher when he said all your sins are forgiven. But when you get out there into the world to live your life, the Devil beats you black and blue with that old thing that you did back there, because somehow it still seems like you are somewhat who you used to be. *You don't see yourself as a new creation.*

> *"If you trust in Jesus Christ's finished work alone for salvation, you are not who you were. You are who God says you are."*

Maybe you really just see yourself as a mildly reformed version of who you used to be. And I'm telling you that *this is not biblical* and *it is not right*. If you trust in Jesus Christ's finished work alone for salvation, *you are not who you were*. You are who God says you are. It's the *world* that says you are who you were in the past.

LIE OF THE WORLD #2: YOU ARE YOUR PRESENT PERFORMANCE

It's also the world, not God, that says you can fill in the blank for your identity, namely, know who you are by how you perform in the *present*. So, according to the world, if you do good stuff, you're a good guy. If you do bad stuff, you're a bad guy. If you do good stuff, you're a good woman. If you do bad stuff, you're a bad woman. That's where we get "performanced-based identity," which we try to synthesize into "performance-based Christianity" (which is not Christianity at all).

That's why maybe you haven't prayed this week, because that worldly thinking has gotten into your mind. You're thinking, "Man, I'm not going to pray. Why should I? I really blew it last week. God doesn't want to hear from me! I mean, I'd love to go pray, but God doesn't want to hear my prayers because I sure have been messing up." You're living as if your performance is what gains you access into the prayer closet or the throne room of God. The fact of the matter is, the reason we can "boldly approach the throne of Grace and find help in our time of need" (Hebrews 4:16) is not because I did a great job, it's because Jesus did a *perfect* job 2,000 years ago. My identity is determined by His finished work, by His track record, and I enter that throne room in prayer by the blood of Jesus. When I've blundered the most is when I need to pray the most. He wants to hear me the most in my times of failure and weakness.

But, listen, we do this to each other—even in the church. Consider how we talk about people. "Hey, I don't like that person over there."

"Really? Why not?"

"Because, don't you know? He's a jerk!" In other words, I'm going to fill in the blank on their identity based on how they have treated me. That is the world's way, *"but this is not the way you learned Christ"* (Eph. 4:20).

If you do it to others, I can just about guarantee you're doing it to yourself as well. It's performance-driven identification. It's the false but subtle belief: "You are what you do."

LIE OF THE WORLD #3: YOU ARE WHAT OTHERS SAY, THINK, OR BELIEVE YOU ARE

Here's another one: the world says you are who you are based on what other people say or think about you. For many of us, there's somebody at your school, somebody in your family, or somebody or a group of "somebodies" out there somewhere else in your life, and it's what they think about you that matters the most to you. It's like, "Man, if they think I'm cool, then I'm cool. If they think I'm a jerk, I must be a jerk. If they think I'm great, then I'm great. But, if they think I'm terrible, I'm terrible." And so, you let their opinions become the filter for what you do or don't do, say or don't say, wear or don't wear. (That's why we spend money we don't have to buy things we don't need to impress people we don't like!) What they think matters too much! And mark it down; the world reinforces daily that what others think matters.

So, if you get a lot of likes on social media today, you're happy. And if somebody makes one negative comment among the twenty you get, you're sad and depressed for three days because you think you're worth and your value is tied to that. This makes it pretty easy for Satan. The Devil can influence any of that on any given day. His strategy keeps your sense of value constantly changing, as even the people themselves who are determining that value are changing from day to day and moment to moment.

But do you know who "the big ones" are when it comes to the "they" and the "those people" in your life? I'm talking about the "*them*," the people whose opinions seem to affect our behavior and thinking the most. Mom and Dad.

You may be like many who will read this who didn't grow up in a home like I grew up in—a home where they told you that you are a blessing from God, where they believed in your potential and reminded you of their love and support verbally and in countless other ways. You may have grown up in a home where you were told things like, "You're in the way," "You're an inconvenience or nuisance," "You cost too much," "You're a mistake," and "You break everything you put your hands on." You were called by your given name but also many others, like: dummy, idiot, stupid, retard, and maybe worse. And now here you are, a grown adult perhaps, and maybe your mom and dad aren't alive anymore, but they're still living, rent-free, in your head and having daily conversations about you.

You know when you'll see it the most? This might be a decent example. Let's say you're going through an average day, and you make a mistake—and I don't mean some moral failure. I mean a goof or blunder. Maybe you just broke your glasses or dropped a plate on the floor. Yet, all of a sudden, it's like a dam breaks in your soul. Your limbic system kicks in, adrenaline and cortisol start shooting through your body, and very old identity thoughts flood your head and start coming out of your mouth. You begin to say things like, "I'm such an idiot. I'm so stupid." As a matter of fact, you're using some of the same phrases that your parents used. "I can't believe this, man. I'm a waste of the breath I'm taking in! My mom was right! My dad was right! I'm a mistake! I'll never amount to anything! This proves it! Every day, I'm reminded that I'm a waste of time and space! Oh, God!" Think about it: *All of a sudden, you've begun to say things out of your own mouth that God would never say about you.*

"The World should never be allowed to tell us who we are."

Let me tell you something: *Those thoughts didn't come from God.* They come from your *flesh,* magnified by the *World* because those thoughts are defining your identity along completely different lines than God.

The fact of the matter is that *we are not to listen to the world.* What does the Bible say? The Bible says in Romans 12:1-2, *"Do not be conformed to the world."* The world is not allowed to tell us who we are. The world is not allowed to define our identity. But if it does, then we're being conformed to the world.

It works like this: If we let the world tell us who we are, and our beliefs determine our behavior, and the me I see is the me I'll be, then guess what? The world is ultimately determining my life's output. I'm going to love what the world loves. I'm going to pursue what the world pursues. I'm going to behave how the world behaves. I'm going to do that because the world is defining my identity, even though the Bible says, "Do not be conformed to the world."

But here's the other side of that truth from the Word: "but be transformed." Then it tells us how: "by the renewing of your mind." There it is again: **the way you get transformation on the outside is by getting transformation from the inside, and that's why God is renewing our mind.** He's renewing our mind to agree with Him, to think like Him, to see life and situations and people how God sees them. Why? Because He's tackling identity. *We are new creatures in Jesus.* The world doesn't get to tell us who we are. Why? Because God has spoken on the issue! Debate over! Your identity is settled in Christ!

◆◆◆◆◆◆◆◆◆◆◆◆◆◆◆◆◆◆◆◆◆◆

PRAYING IT OUT

Father, I love You today. Thank You for every heartbeat in my chest. I give You all of my regrets and promises that didn't work, and I lay them at Your feet. Today, I am taking up my new identity in Jesus. I am trusting that I am who You say I am, and I want to live like it. Father, by Your Holy Spirit, give me the faith to believe that all I once was has been crucified with Christ. Give me also the faith to believe that my performance does not determine who I really am. And help me not to cling to, nor orient my life around the opinions of others. It's only Your opinion of me that counts. You say I am loved and accepted unconditionally and eternally. Fix my thoughts on the truth and take captive every thought raised against the knowledge of God.

I pray strategically that I would surrender to You, trust You, and put all of my weight onto Your Word, knowing it will hold me, knowing that it will not break. God help me to live as if this is true because it is. May the Devil know the difference. May I live the difference; may others see the difference, because You are great, and You're good, and You are living in me. Help me to lean on all that You are for my life, I pray—in Jesus' Name. Amen.

LIVING IT OUT

Letting God define who you are and really believing and receiving it fully is everything. If you aren't sure, you will spend your whole life trying to find your identity through performance and people. Do you struggle to remember that God has defined who you are? What other activities, actions, things, and people are you letting define you? Really consider the things that you care about the most, what you think about when you stop thinking about everything else, or what makes you the most fearful or excited. This can help you to pinpoint some things you are looking at that you feel give your life meaning or identity. What God wants to do is form Christ in you, and He has already defined a new identity for you through the finished work of Christ. Begin to read more of the New Testament letters, paying careful attention to how much of it focuses on identity. Memorize and remind yourself of the truths that touch your heart and assure you of who Christ has said you are now.

CHAPTER 4
THE OVERCOMER'S IDENTITY: A NEW CREATION

"God loves you just the way you are, but He refuses to leave you that way. He wants you to be just like Jesus."
— Max Lucado

"The only identity that cannot be taken away from us is the identity given to us by God."
— Timothy Keller

Let's consider an example to begin to understand just how much belief determines behavior. There's a young man, a junior in college, who is grossly overweight. He only likes two things in life: girls and key lime pie. So, how might he sum up his identity? His identity is: "I'm a hormone with an appetite," right? One day he's in the cafeteria at college polishing off a piece of key lime pie when all of a sudden a pretty little cheerleader in a miniskirt goes traipsing across in front of where he's eating. He pushes aside his empty plate and begins to follow her out the door, down the steps, and across the quad on the campus. Now, he's really after her. Running hard. His heart is practically beating out of his chest.

About then, the track coach of his college sees him running after this girl and thinks, "Man, for that kid's size, he's fast." (Of course, he's motivated.) The coach manages to stop this young man and says, "Young man, y'know, for your size, you're fast. Have you ever run track before?" The coach could see the incredulous look on the young man's face. "No man, I'm serious. I really think you've got talent. What year are you?"

The young man answers, dumbfounded. "I'm a junior."

The coach gets excited, "Okay. Would you run for me next year? Just go out for track, and I promise you'll make the team." So the kid goes out for track, and sure enough, he makes it. Then, he submits himself to the coach's training program. He starts losing weight and picking up speed. He also discovers the breadth of his untapped talent for running. Before long, he's faster than he ever imagined. And he loves it. It's clear that he's got a gift. It's unbelievable. His life has changed. He's winning track meets, week after week, and he lives for the sport. It's the most amazing time of his life so far.

So now, let's fast forward. One year after the cheerleader-chasing incident, he's on the sidelines of the track, stretching for the next relay, when all of a sudden that same cheerleader (the same one he'd been chasing one year prior) walks up to the fence. And guess what? In her hand, she's holding—a piece of key lime pie! She flutters her long eyelashes, curling her finger towards herself, and calls out to him, "Hey, Big Boy—come over here." He goes over to her, curious. She says, "Hey, listen, if you will leave this running thing you're doing and come with me, you can have this piece of pie. And you can have the rest of the pie it was cut from. And—you can have—me, too."

He doesn't bat an eye before answering. "What? No way."

Incredulous, she questions *"No way*?! What do you mean?"

He says, "You don't understand. I'm not the guy I was last year. I'm a runner now. I didn't come here to leave with you. I came here to win this race. Bye."

Catch this: All of a sudden, he's exercising a new authority in his choices because his identity is no longer, "I'm a hormone with an appetite." His identity has changed. Now, he can say, "I'm a runner who wins, and that is what I'm designed by God to do, and that affects everything else."

Can you see how your sense of identity is at the core of nearly every choice you make in life?

I recently read the book, *Atomic Habits*, by James Clear. I encourage you to read it; it's a great book. What's amazing is that he's puts forth so much of the science about how one's sense of identity influences the habits of his life. Mr. Clear shared these ideas in 2019, but God's been telling us this for 2,000 years. Please understand, if you have the Word of God, you're not behind the times—you're ahead of the times, and fit for the times. The Bible says what we believe about our identity matters and it shows up in our life.

Even the word "believe," comes from two words: "be" and "live." You live the way you live because of who you see yourself to be. Again, "The Me I see is the Me I'll be!"

WE HAVE A SOFTWARE PROBLEM

One day years ago, sitting down at my computer, I had just completed a newsletter we were about to print for our ministry. Now, the newsletter looked right on the screen of my computer. But I have discovered something about desktop publishers. You don't know what you have until you hit "print." So, I hit print, and it came out as gobbledygook. You couldn't even discern the difference between the pictures and the text. I assumed my printer was having problems and tried printing from a different app. The other app printed fine, so I knew it wasn't the printer. Not really sure what was going on, I did a bit of research and found out the answer pretty quickly. (Thank you, Google.)

What I learned was this. Out of all the apps in cyberspace and out of all the printers in "printerdom," they all work fine. They communicate fine, they input-output fine, but when it came to *this* particular program and *this* particular printer, there was something involved called a "virus." I guess you've heard that term before, right?

So, it wasn't a *hardware* problem, it was a *software* problem. It's the way the computer was *thinking* about the problem. It wasn't the keyboard, the cable, the printer, drum, jet, or anything *physically* broken. It was just an issue with the way the computer was *processing information.*

What is a computer virus, anyway? A computer virus is a batch of *bad code* (bad *information*) that has worked its way onto the hard drive and is *corrupting the output.*

What do you have to do to fix it? You have to download something known as a "patch" or a "fix." That's what I had to do to fix my newsletter printing issues. I had to download a patch and update the software. A *patch* is a batch of *corrected* code—*true code that is designed by the manufacturer to replace the bad code.* No one has to send a tech to your house to come and mess with the computer machine. You just have to download the right code to replace the wrong code—the truth to replace the lie—because they understand that as soon as you get the truth to replace the lie, this *automatically corrects the output* by default. Are you tracking with me here?

That's how it is with us. Why do we have the output we don't want? Because every day we're involved in social media, we're going to our job, we're watching television, we're having conversations with people, and basically, **the world, the flesh, and the Devil are putting viruses on the hard drives of our souls to get their output, not the good things God wants to produce.** And that is why we need to daily expose ourselves to www dot B-I-B-L-E dot com and download the Truth of who we are in Christ. When we download the truth, that truth replaces a lie, and when the truth replaces a lie, it automatically corrects our output. Can you see that?

*"When we download the truth, it replaces
a lie, and when the truth replaces a lie,
it automatically corrects our output."*

Please understand that God is trying to get the truth into you so that you understand what He says about you, not what the world says. **The only way to immunize yourself against error is to know the truth**—God's truth about who you are in Jesus.

I'm not who I was in the past. I'm not how I perform in the present. I'm not my mistakes. I'm not my regrets. I'm not my sins. I'm not, *I'm not,* **I'm not**. I'm not even what people think about me. I am who God says I am, and God defines our identity entirely by our union with Jesus.

When we "uplink" to Romans 6:3-5, we "download" our identity in Jesus. This is who you are in Jesus: I'm going to give you three truths about your identity.

However, I'll warn you: As we walk through these three things, you might be doing so as a born-again believer. And in spite of that, the following things that God says are true of you will not *feel* like they are true as we go through them. The Devil will sit on your shoulder like a prosecuting attorney and give you a list of reasons from last week that say this *cannot* be true for you, and you will be tempted to start an argument with God. Take my advice—don't start an argument with God, because he hasn't ever lost one. *This is* who you are in Jesus.

Now, if you're *not* saved by the grace of Jesus Christ alone through faith in His perfect life, sacrificial death, and overcoming resurrection from the dead, then the following is not true about you. If you don't know Jesus as your Lord and Savior, these are not true about you, but the good news is in front of you right now, and you can walk underneath that exit sign. You can give your life to Jesus, and this can be true about you today. But if you're saved by grace and born again of the Spirit of God, then these things are true about you *now*. It's not about *feel*, it's by *faith*. This is who you are in Jesus.

IDENTITY TRUTH #1—YOU ARE SOMEONE WHO HAS DIED WITHCHRIST

First of all, if you're saved by grace, born again of the Spirit of God, then you are a person who died with Christ on that cross.

Look at Romans 6:2: *"Certainly not, how shall we who **died** (past tense!) **to sin** live any longer in it?"*

And verse three says, *"Do you not know that as many of us as were baptized into Christ Jesus were baptized into his **death**."*

Verse five tells us: *"For if we've been united together in the likeness of his **death**…"*

Then look at verse six: *"Knowing this, that our old self **was crucified** with him, so that the body of sin might be done away with."* Why? *"So that we should no longer be slaves of sin."*

How could this not be clear? You're a person who has died, with Jesus, when Jesus died on the cross!

Here is a tip: When Satan brings up all those sins that you've committed, remind him of these verses! As someone has said, "Next time the Devil comes to remind you of your past, remind him of his future!"

Sometimes someone will come up to me after a church service where I'll be preaching and say, "Please pray for me, Scott. I'm struggling in an area of my life, but, I'm working *toward the victory*…"

To him, I'll say: "Friend, we are not working *toward* victory, we are working *from* victory. The victory has already been won!"

When was the victory won? On the cross of Jesus, two thousand years ago. Now, we merely enforce the video he secured!

IDENTITY TRUTH #2—YOU ARE SOMEONE WHO WAS BURIED WITH CHRIST

You're a person who is buried with Jesus. Verse four of Romans 6 says, "We *were buried with Him* through baptism into death." Paul brings up baptism. Let's camp there a second and allow me to ask you a question. Does baptism save you? No, that would be salvation by works, if it did. The thief on the cross to whom Jesus said, "Today you'll be with me in Paradise" was not baptized—yet he still went to Paradise, obviously. You read all through the Scripture, and you'll find that the theology of baptism and salvation is very clear: We're saved by grace through faith, not by works. Baptism is a sign. It's an outward sign of an inward work. It doesn't save us any more than the wedding ring I wear makes me married. The wedding ring doesn't make me married, but it shows people I am married. So, baptism shows people you're saved, but you're not saved by baptism.

Let me ask you another question. Do people getting baptized just need a sprinkling of water, or do you take them all the way under? You take them under. (I've always said, "You don't get saved in spots, so you ought not to just get wet in spots!") *You take them under.* Why? Because that's how Jesus got baptized and that is what the Greek word *baptizō* means—"to immerse." When someone gets baptized, the person doing the baptizing quotes a verse, saying, "You're united with Him in the likeness of His death," and that's when you get in the water. And then he says, "You're buried with Him in baptism and raised to walk in newness of life." Literally, he quotes these verses we are studying right now.

Now, someone says, "Well, baptism is just a symbol." Okay, do you want to know what it really symbolizes? Next time your pastor baptizes someone, tell him to hold them under for 45 minutes. You know what this means, then, right? They're dead if that happens! Baptism "symbolizes" our true spiritual union with Christ in His death!

> *"You were buried with Jesus, and now anything the Devil can bring up is something God says is in the grave."*

So, we have died with Jesus, and we're buried. Because you *bury* what has *died*. On the cross, Jesus did not faint; he did not swoon; he did not fall asleep; he *died*—and that's why they buried him. In the same way, your old self was crucified with Jesus. And also, on top of that, you were buried with Jesus, and I'm telling you that anything the Devil can remind you of about your "old self" is something God says is in the grave. Hallelujah!

IDENTITY TRUTH #3—YOU ARE SOMEONE WHO WAS RAISED WITH CHRIST

Lastly, you were raised with Jesus. Romans 6:4 says, "We were raised with Jesus to walk in newness of life." As Romans 8:11 says, *"...the Spirit of Him who raised Jesus from the dead dwells in you..."* No, I haven't finished reading the verse, it does say more, but that one line—wow—that one line changes everything. Since "the Spirit of Him who raised Jesus from the dead *is living in you...*" Did you get that? He's living inside of you! And He's living inside of you in the face of every temptation, in the face of every depression, in the face of every opposition, despite the best that the Devil can bring! The Spirit of Him who raised Jesus from the dead is resident within you! That is no small reality!

Then it continues, "[If] He raised Christ from the dead, will He not also give life to your mortal bodies through His spirit that lives in you?" In other words, won't He also give you life as you walk around in this body? Won't He also do what He has to do and work what He has to work? *"It is God who works in you both to will and to do for His good pleasure"* (Phil. 2:13). The Bible amplifies this truth about us in other places as well. 2 Corinthians 5:17—*"If anyone is in Christ, he is a new creation."* He did not say, "hopes to be" a new creation, or "might be" a new creation, or "perhaps if he learns enough Bible verses, goes to enough conferences, attends church enough, or goes to seminary and gets the degree, then he'll be a new creation." No, through Christ, it's an established fact. If you're saved, you are a brand-new creature. And to make sure we don't misunderstand him, Paul goes ahead and inserts the fine print: *"...old things have passed away; behold, all things have become new."* It's a done deal! Your new identity equals "new creature in Christ!"

SINNER OR SAINT?

So, what does the Bible say about you? If you ask the average believer to tell you about their walk with Jesus, they'll say, "Well, y'know, I'm just a sinner saved by grace."

To that I say, "You had better be careful." Why? Because "The me I see is the me I'll be." My beliefs determine my behavior. What I know determines how I go. And you're saying "I am just a sinner?!"

You might be thinking now, "Wait a minute, isn't that right, though? We are just sinners saved by grace, right?" Yes, yes it's true—in terms of earning salvation. It's true in terms of meriting heaven. Yes, if you get salvation or heaven at all, it's because you are saved by grace. You're a sinner saved by grace. Yes, but, here's what I have found: When you go through the New Testament, for every one time that Christians are referred to as "sinners" in the New Testament, they're called "saints" ten times as often. "So what do you deduce from that, Watson?"

"For every one time that a Christian is referred to as a sinner in the New Testament, they're called saints ten times as often."

Let it really sink in. God calls His people *saints* versus *sinners* ten to one. You may say, "Why is that important?" Here's why that's important. Because the Me I see is the Me I'll be. If I get out of bed in the morning, and I walk around saying, "I'm just a sinner saved by grace... I'm just a sinner... just a sinner... *just a sinner*," then guess what I'm going to do? I'm going to sin, sin, sin until the cows come home. And do you know what else I'm going to do? I'm going to justify it the whole time! And if somebody calls me on it, I'll say, "Well, of course I'm sinning! That's what sinners do, right?!"

What if, instead—*regardless* of my feelings about it—I start agreeing with God? "*I'm a saint!*" My feet hit the floor in the morning and, bam! First thought! *I'm a saint!* Hallelujah! *I'm a saint in Jesus.* Glory to God! *I'm a new creation. Old things are passed away, behold, all things become brand new!* Instead of confessing that I'm a sinner, I start confessing that I'm a saint. Remember, my beliefs determine my behavior. Just by believing, by really embracing that I'm a saint in God, I will, by default, live a more saintly life.

Satan doesn't want you to know what a "saint" is. He wants us to misdefine it. Satan wants you to believe that a saint means "dead Catholic." Then you're likely disqualified on at least one count, if not two right now! But here is the truth: A saint is *anybody saved by grace.* Anybody who has Christ living within them. Anybody who has given their lives to Jesus for salvation. I don't care if you've been saved for five minutes or 50 years, God says you're a saint!

My own, self-generated "righteous" deeds are like filthy rags before God—there's no access to sainthood for me through them at all! Listen, if Jesus lives inside of you, you're a saint. If your name is written in the Lamb's Book of Life, you're a saint.

So, if you are those things, the question is not *whether you are* a saint, the question is: Do you believe it? Will you function in it? Will you embrace it? You may be thinking, "But I committed crimes." That doesn't mean you're a criminal. Perhaps you are thinking, "But I was promiscuous!" That doesn't mean you're identity is a whore. I could go on and on, but here is the point: **You're not defined by your sin.** You're not defined by your addiction. You're not defined by your past. You're not defined by what people say. **You're defined by God's Word, and God says you're a person who died with Jesus, who was buried with Jesus, and who was raised with Jesus!**

HOW TO LIVE THE SAINT LIFE

Will you believe God and take Him at His Word? I'm telling you, *it will change things.* Before today is done, you will face the same temptation that's been dragging you in the ditch for weeks, months, or years—you will, it's waiting for you. But what if instead of giving in like you always have, you looked temptation in the eye and said, "I will not give in to you. I will not obey you. I will not submit to you. And here's why, because *that's not who I am anymore!*"

If you still don't believe me, let me share an important point: Even the most carnal, ungodly church members in the New Testament—the Corinthians—*even they were called "saints."* Listen, it was bad with the Corinthians. They had chaos in their worship services; if anybody said anything in church, it was for their own edification, not the edification of the body. And as soon as they'd leave church, they would go out and hook up with temple prostitutes in a pagan temple. They even had one guy in the church that Paul referred to as a "brother"—that means he was a saved person—who was sleeping with his stepmother! And to *that church* in the first three verses, he calls them "saints." Why? Because sainthood is not determined by how I'm living. Sainthood is not determined by what I've done. Sainthood is not determined by my failure. It is determined by a union with Jesus. And, so important, the reason he wrote to them the letter of 1 Corinthians was to remind them they were saints, to rebuke them over the fact that their lifestyle was incongruent with their new identity!

So, I remind you who you are. You're a saint. *Live* like a saint and *think* like a saint, because God said you *are* a saint. The me I see is the me I'll be. There is victory waiting for you here!

I don't know about you, but there are some things from last year that I don't want to drag into the next. I've been kicked around, beat up, pushed down, and I'm telling you, I want this year to be different. And if God says that the only way I'm going to do that is by understanding and believing in who I am, then that's what I want to do.

A FUNNY STORY TO WRAP UP THIS THOUGHT

A drill sergeant came to his platoon as they were about to go through battle maneuvers, and said, "Guys, we're going to go through battle maneuvers. There's only one catch." The men looked up, curious. "We have no weapons: no grenades, no tanks, nothing. We don't even have blanks for the guns. We've had some cutbacks around here."

So the platoon members replied, "How are we going to do battle maneuvers if we don't have stuff we would do battle with?"

The sergeant had a ready answer: "When we split into two teams, you're going to *pretend* you have grenades and guns and knives. If you want to throw a grenade, pull your empty hand back behind your head in throwing position and scream, 'lob, lob,' and you'll be lobbing a grenade. If you want to shoot a rifle, just put your hands up like you're holding one—empty as they are—and just say, 'bang, bang, bang' good and loud. If you want to use a knife, we don't have knives, but if you just say, 'jab, jab, jab,' that's your knife."

So, they split into two teams, and there was one soldier rehearsing his weapons, "lob, lob, bang, bang, jab, jab, lob, lob, bang, bang, jab, jab." He looked across at the other team, and there was another soldier from the other side coming at him full steam, and he thought, "What would I do in battle? Oh, right, I'd throw a grenade!" So he tossed emptiness into the air as he shouted, "lob, lob!" but the guy kept on trucking. The soldier assumed the other fellow didn't hear him, so he jumped up from the trench shouting, "bang, bang, bang!" but the guy was *still* coming full steam towards him.

Finally, he leaped out of the trench, taking his empty hand as he was close enough to touch the other soldier, and yelled, "jab, jab, jab!" The guy was still all over him, so he pushed him off, angry. "Wait a minute; wait a minute; you're not playing right," the first soldier said.

The other man replied innocently, "What do you mean?"

The first guy was getting furious now. "I said, 'lob, lob,' and that's a grenade, so you should have blown up. I said, 'bang, bang, bang,'—I know you heard me—and that's a rifle, so you should've fallen down, and I finished the job with, 'jab, jab, jab.' How more obvious can it get? What is your problem?"

The guy just looked back and said, "rumble, rumble. I'm a tank."

What's the takeaway here? The *me I see is the me I'll be.* Maybe as you're reading this book you've been saying, "lob, lob, bang,

bang, jab, jab," when it's time to say, "rumble, rumble; look out Devil, here I come." You can say to that enemy, "Devil, I'm not who you say I am. I'm not who the world says I am. I'm not caught up in the systems of this world. Rumble, rumble, I'm the tank! **I'm defined by a higher standard, and that is who God says I am in Jesus. I'm a new creation. I'm born again. I'm a saint in God by grace!"**

"God wants to parade you through this culture as a trophy of His grace and a living letter to be read by men."

Here's your invitation right now, from God to you. Right now, I'm asking you to rise above what people think. I'm asking you to get your mind off everything else except one thing, and that is what God has said to you today and why He said it. God wants to parade you through this culture as a trophy of His grace and a living letter to be read by men. He wants to show you off as the change and the joy that He brings to a life. And I'm telling you, they won't see it right if you and I don't live it right. But the way we live it right is by getting it right, right here and now, by saying and believing, "Lord, I want to be what you said I am. You say I am a saint. I'm an overcomer! I'm more than a conqueror! I'm a new creation. Rumble, rumble, Devil here I come!"

✦✦✦✦✦✦✦✦✦✦✦✦✦✦✦✦✦✦✦✦

PRAYING IT OUT

Heavenly Father, I'm thankful that Your Word determines reality. Thank You for speaking over me and changing the very nature of my being. Thank You for making me a new creation. As your Word says, "We are created in Christ Jesus for good works, which God prepared beforehand for us to walk in." Make my heart lean on this truth. Jesus, build my life on the reality that You have destroyed all that once was and raised up a new creation through Your life, death, and resurrection. I fully embrace today that my old self was crucified with Christ and that it was buried, too. I thank You that I've been raised up with Jesus to walk as a brand new life.

I no longer want the life I used to have. I only want the life that You are living through me. Jesus, have Your way. I surrender all. Please take me as I am, but don't leave me where I've been. Take me into a future of overcoming, because "the victory that has overcome the world is our faith!" In Jesus' Name, I pray. Amen.

LIVING IT OUT

Do you struggle with allowing the world to define you, who you are? Have you embraced your new identity in Christ? Everyone struggles to believe the truth sometimes, but you want to move towards a place where your struggle is a victorious struggle, where the norm is that you win most of the time. You want to live out of your new identity so that God can live in you and love through you. How often do you tell yourself the truth about yourself? It may sound odd, but you have to preach this truth to yourself, in your head, in your prayers through thanksgiving, and out loud at times. Gather some scriptures, starting with those used in the last two chapters perhaps, and read them each day until they sink in and you begin to see them showing up in your difficult moments when you feel insecure about who you are. Over time, you'll begin to believe the truth rather than the lie.

CHAPTER 5
THE OVERCOMER'S INHERITANCE: CLAIMING KINGDOM RIGHTS

"To be a Christian is to be a freedom fighter
and to love every form of freedom."
– Martin Luther

As we continue to discover how our understanding of our identity shapes our daily lives in Christ, we are going to stay in Romans chapter six. We're talking about overcoming defeat patterns. As we've been saying, all of us know what it's like when we sin on this side of salvation. We also know that dreaded cycle that can so easily develop, those repeated patterns of more sin, resulting in struggle, doubt, confusion, regret.

"'Victory in Jesus' can be a daily reality for you as a child of God."

So we wonder how to escape the cycle. For a while, we do all kinds of things to deal with it. We start New Year's resolutions committed to breaking the habit; we pray and make promises to God that we're not going to do it anymore; we bring in accountability partners; or we read books on "12 steps to stopping" whatever-your-struggle-is, and what we discover is, that rarely works. So we find ourselves making excuses for our sins. But what we are trying to understand here is how God gave you a brand new identity.

Good news: "Victory in Jesus" is not just the Baptist national anthem. It's not just a song. It's not just a bumper sticker. *It can be a daily reality for you* as a child of God. **God intends to infuse victory into every area of your life. There is not a single area of your life that God wants you resigned to defeat. He wants you to live the overcoming Christian life!**

So how do you break those cycles of defeat? The first thing Paul tackles in Romans 6 is identity. You have to know who you are in Christ. We discussed that in the last chapter three. Why is it important? Because the *me I see is the me I'll be*. You can't just change habits. You can't truly change behavior until you first change your perspective on your identity, until you first understand who you are. So the first thing that he tells them is who they are in Christ.

But next, let's be reminded of what Paul says in Romans 6:7 after he says, "we should no longer be slaves of sin"—watch this—

> *"because he who has died has been freed from sin. Now if we died with Christ, we believe that we shall also live with Him, knowing that Christ, having been raised from the dead, dies no more. Death no longer has dominion over Him. For the death that He died, He died to sin once for all; but the life that He lives, He lives to God. Likewise, you also reckon yourselves to be dead indeed to sin, but alive to God in Christ Jesus our Lord. Therefore, do not let sin reign in your mortal body, that you should obey it in its lusts. And do not present your members as instruments of unrighteousness to sin, but present yourselves to God as being alive from the dead and your members as instruments of righteousness to God. For sin shall not have dominion over you, for you are not under law but under grace."*

So he told you *who you are* in Christ, but **if you're going to break those defeat cycles, you also need to know *what you have* in Christ.** You need to understand the inheritance available to you through the finished work of Christ.

Here's what I've found: you won't *use* what you have in Jesus if you don't *know* what you have in Jesus. That's just common sense. You won't *employ* what you have in Christ or *enjoy* what you have in Christ if you don't *know* what you have in Christ.

I once heard a story about a fellow who wanted to go on a cruise so badly, he saved his money for ages to go. He didn't make a lot of money, but he wanted to go on a cruise. So he finally got enough money to buy the tickets and stepped onto his first ever cruise ship. Now, the thing about cruises I've noticed is when people come back from a cruise, they're not talking about the shuffleboard. They're not talking about how deep the pool was on the third deck. They're talking about *food*. They say it's unbelievable. There's all-you-can-eat breakfast. There's all-you-can-eat lunch. There's all-you-can-eat dinner. And as if that wasn't enough, there's a midnight buffet! (A sermon on gluttony on one of those Christian cruises would go over like a screen door on a submarine!)

> *"You won't use what you have in Jesus if you don't know what you have in Jesus."*

So anyway, this guy got on a cruise ship, and there were breakfast buffets, lunch buffets, dinner buffets, and there were even midnight buffets. But every time the smorgasbord was put out, this guy was absent. His friends were wondering where on earth he could be. He was missing the best part of the trip! They decided that the next time the dinner bell rang, they weren't going to go eat. Instead, they were going to go look for him and tell him where he should be. And so they did. The next time dinner came, everybody was getting in line to eat, and they went the other way. They went searching all over the boat, and at long last finally found this old boy in his cabin sitting on the end of his bunk eating a pack of Lay's cheese crackers.

His friends said, "What in the world are you doing in here?!"

The man answered, apologetically, "I don't mean to be anti-social; you know how badly I wanted to go on this trip. So I saved my money and saved some more. And when I finally got enough money to buy the ticket, I just bought the ticket and got on the boat with you guys. I never got around to saving the money to buy food once I got on the boat."

They stared at him, dumbfounded, for a moment, before one of them said, "The food comes with the trip!"

He was missing a key piece of information. Was he not? It seems obvious, but I just described so many Christians all over our country today. They're going to church on Sundays, they have the Jesus shirt, and they have the big Bible in their dresser, but they're struggling to walk out this faith, and they don't understand what's wrong. Here's why: because they don't understand that when Jesus died, he didn't just die to buy the ticket for the trip. He bought the whole buffet, too! He's not just getting you on the boat to heaven. He's given you victory here and now!

Now, I want to ask *you*: what are you doing? **Don't you know the spread that's out here for you on the journey with Jesus?** Gosh, I do. Not entirely, perhaps, but the more I grow, the more I see it. I don't know about you, but I want to know what I have in Jesus!

Following are three things we have in Christ. For the first, let's look again at Romans 6:6: "...knowing this, that our old man (that is, our old self) was crucified with him, that the body of sin might be done away with." Do you hear that? "...done away with, so that we should no longer be slaves to sin." What did he just say? We are no longer slaves to sin!

TRANSFORMATIONAL TRUTH #1—YOU HAVE FREEDOM IN CHRIST

So, here is truth number one: you're not a slave to sin. You have freedom in the Lord Jesus Christ. According to Romans 6, **by virtue of your union with Jesus in his death, burial, and resurrection, you have freedom in Jesus.**

Now, I'm not saying that you'll live above sin. There's sin in our flesh; that's just how it is. We live in a world system that tempts us all the time. So, I'm not teaching that we can live above sin, and the Bible doesn't either. Not at all. But I am telling you that we have something on this side of giving our heart to Jesus that we did not have on the other side when we were under our old master—we have a *choice*. **We have a choice because we have freedom in Jesus.** How do we have freedom? Verse seven says, "...because he who has **died** has been freed from sin." You might be thinking, "Scott, are you saying I died?" Yes. I'm saying you died because the Word of God is saying that. When did that death happen? When Jesus died on the cross. You died when He died, as verse eight reveals, "...we died **with** Christ. Since we died with Christ, we believe that we shall also live with him."

Remember, your union with Christ was complete. So verse nine is true of you when it speaks of Christ. Verse nine continues: ..."knowing that Christ, having been raised from the dead, dies no more. Death no longer has dominion over him." **So mark this: death has no dominion over you either, because you died when he died.** Verse 10 finishes: "The death that he died, he died to sin once for all, and the life that he lives, he lives to God." Likewise, you and I, redeemed, united with Christ, and having his Holy Spirit, we live to God!

> *"We have a choice because we have freedom in Jesus."*

Perhaps you still don't get it. Here's a story to help you out. A man was once drafted to fight in Napoleon's army. He didn't want to fight, but he had to submit to the draft. Now here's the thing: he had a friend who hadn't been drafted who had always wanted to fight for Napoleon's army. So when he was drafted, his first thought was to bring his friend. He went down to the draft office and said, "Listen, I know I've been drafted and you want me to fight in the army. I get it. But I have a friend here who has not been drafted. He would love to fight. Can he go in my place?" They said yes, so his friend submitted to the draft in his place. For two years he fought for Napoleon until he was one day killed in battle.

A few years went by, and through some clerical error, the original guy was drafted a second time. He went to the drafting office and said boldly, "You can't draft me."

They were mystified, of course. "And why not?" they asked, incredulously.

His answer was sure. "Because I'm dead."

They laughed, replying, "Well, you're standing right here, and you look like you're fit for military service to us! Are you crazy? Why are you saying you're dead?"

He just pointed, "Look in the book." So they did, and they saw something that they'd never seen. There was the man's name as officially drafted, then crossed out, and beside his name was written the name of his friend who had fought in his place. And beside the friend's name was inscribed the date that he was killed in battle. So the fellow repeated himself. "See? You can't draft me."

They did not understand. The debate became so heated that it went all the way to Emperor Napoleon himself. So there they were, Napoleon with the recruiters and draft log open, and they were explaining, "Sir, we're trying to do our job. This man is in good fighting order. He could fight for your army. We don't understand this idea that he can't be drafted. We've never seen this before. Could you please decide? Can we draft him or not?"

Napoleon looked at the book, then looked back at them and said, "He's right. We can't draft him. This man has already submitted to the draft *through a substitute*. This man has already fought in my army *through a substitute*. This man has already died for his country *through a substitute*. And *a man who has died once cannot die twice. Therefore, the draft law has no claim on his life."*

Do you know where I'm going with this? **God united me with Jesus on the cross 2,000 years ago, put me in a tomb with Jesus 2,000 years ago, and when Jesus came out, I came out as a new creation united with Jesus.** I have freedom in Christ. Death has no claim on me! Sin has no claim on me, nor does it have a claim on you! If you're saved, then death has lost its sting! Hallelujah! The grave has been emptied of its power, because we are united with Jesus, and Jesus is alive, and we can live a new life in freedom. Friend, I'm telling you—we have freedom in Jesus!

TRANSFORMATIONAL TRUTH #2—YOU HAVE RIGHTS IN CHRIST

The second thing we have in Jesus is a set of rights. Now, it's not as obvious here in this passage as it is in other areas of scripture, so we are going to go to Galatians where the same author is writing on the subject more directly. Listen to what Paul says in Galatians 4:4-5, 7. "...*when the fullness of the time had come, God sent forth His Son, born of a woman, born under the law, to redeem those who were under the law, that we might receive the adoption as sons...Therefore you are no longer a slave but a son."* **Jesus purchased us out of slavery (the literal meaning of "redeemed") in order to give us the full rights of sons!** You're no longer under an old master. You're under a new Master. And since you're a son, God has made you also an heir with Christ!

Okay, so what do my rights as a child of God have to do with living my days in victory despite the temptations and struggles that come my way? What do rights have to do with anything? *Everything.* Now this is a tough pill to swallow for us because we come from a Western culture, and the Eastern minds that wrote this book were more integrated in their thinking. In Western thinking, we read the Bible through a more compartmentalized Western lens, and so we don't see it, especially in this area of rights and what that has to do with our daily battles. Well, we do see it—we just don't recognize it.

I'll give you a Western example to show this principle of "rights." Have you ever been watching a football game, and the game stopped? Something happens on the field, a call is made, one of the players disagrees, and so the game stops. Now you have some 6 ft. 5 in., 375lb linebacker in a vicious argument with a 5 ft. 7in., 125lb referee, and man are they *mad*. Now, if you don't know football, you're seeing an argument thinking, *Mr. Referee had better be careful because Mr. Football Player is clearly upset. As a matter of fact, it looks like he's about to lose it. Mr. Referee, if you push it too far, Big Boy might get a little too mad, and it's game over for you.* That would make sense on a surface reading, right?

But if you know the game of football, if you really know how it works, you're actually thinking, *Oh, Mr. Football Player, it's you that had better be careful.* And he is being careful, isn't he? He's mad... but not too mad. I mean he gets loud... but not too loud. He says choice words, and fingers are pointing while spit is flying—but it's flying in the right direction, *away* from the referee—because we understand it's not about *power*. If it was about power, then the player could just punch the referee and it would be game over. But it's not about power; it's about *rights*, and the referee has all the rights!

You see, that football player understands something that is not so readily visible to the naked eye. He knows something about that referee. *In the back pocket of that referee, there's a flag*, and the player knows if he gets too loud, pushes too far, or, God forbid, touches that referee, then oh, man, the worst might happen. That flag might come out of the referee's pocket! And if that flag comes out of that pocket, it doesn't matter how much that player could bench press, how many endorsements he has, or how many touchdowns he's made, he will be sitting down the rest of the night! Because it's not about power. It's about rights. And guess what? The referee has all the rights.

> *"We have something Satan does not have.*
> *We have the rights of a child of God."*

If it was about *power*, then right now today the Devil could walk into the room where you are sitting right now, snap his fingers, and you'd be over with. But I'm going to tell you something: it's not about power, it's about *rights*. We have something he does not have. We have the rights of a child of God. And in the back pocket of every born again child of God, God has put a little yellow flag, and on that flag it says that if you submit yourself to God and you resist the devil, the devil has to flee (James 4:7). It says that God has not given us a spirit of fear, but of power and love and a sound mind (2 Timothy 1:7). In your back pocket, there's a little flag that says that you are more than a conqueror through Him who loved us (Romans 8:37), and listen—"greater is He who is in you than he who is in the world!"

Here's the bottom line: **God has given you all the rights that the Devil does not have, and you can use them.** Listen, the next time the Devil comes to arrest you, *read him your rights*. That's called the Holy Spirit Miranda law. You have rights in Jesus. They'll do you no good, though, if they stay in your back pocket. When's the last time you pulled it out in the face of temptation, or in the face of discouragement or depression? Use your rights!

Now after all that, you might think I'm saying power doesn't matter, but, oh, *it matters.*

That's the third thing: we *do* have power in Jesus. Let's not make it sound like it's irrelevant because it's not. We have power in Jesus. The question is not *whether* we have the power but whether *we know the power that we have.*

Back in the old days when circuses were the major form of entertainment—before insurance liability and all that—you could go up and touch the elephants after the circus. You would just walk around behind the tent, and they'd have four or five elephants lined up. You'd be staring at these massive, four-ton animals with so much power innately within them. Back then they even used the elephants to push those poles up under that canvas when setting up for the circus. There were thousands of seats, and those elephants had to possess a huge amount of strength to do that. It was unbelievable.

So when you'd go around to pet the elephants, they would just be standing there feeding themselves some hay, and, of course, they'd have them restrained. How did they restrain them? Did they have big elephant cages? No. An elephant would have one iron cuff on one of his ankles, and that iron cuff would be hooked up to one iron chain which was hooked to one iron stake, driven into the ground. That's it. And the elephant wouldn't run, he would just stand there, eating. As a matter of fact, he probably had his huge leg swinging lightly as he ate, but every time that chain got taut, he would just ease off—simple as that. When you watch all of this, you're thinking to yourself, "Why is he still here?" The elephant could pull it out, but he doesn't even try—and here's why. When he was a little baby elephant, they brought him in for the first time, stood him right there beside an iron stake, put a cuff on just like that with the same chain.

And what did he do? He did what you expect a baby elephant to do when it realizes it's in bondage. He yanked and pulled and tugged and tugged and yanked and pulled some more—and then... he gave up. He tried his best, but it didn't work. Now the elephant is big. He's been well-fed. He's got plenty of strength now, but when it comes to that chain, he's still in he won't even try to break free. The only frame of reference he has for that chain is this: "When I realized I was chained up, I did my best to break free, and it didn't work. So why even try anymore." The problem is not that he lacks power. The problem is that he does not know the power that he has. He will not use that which he does not know that he has.

By the way, I just described 95% of professing believers in America today. I'm telling you, there are so many of us who are going through the motions, sitting in church seats and singing songs, but we are still in bondage to that chain. And here's what you say to yourself: "When I realized I was chained up, I did everything I could to break free, but it didn't work. So I tried some more, and that didn't work either. I really gave it my best shot. Why even try anymore?"

That is exactly where Satan wants you, and that is *not* where God wants you. God is wanting to deliver truth to your life, as Jesus said, "You shall know the truth, and the truth shall make you free" (John 8:32). The Word of God says you have freedom in Jesus, you have rights in Jesus, and you have power in Jesus. The Devil's demons can't claim that. People far from God can't claim that. But *you can claim that* as a child of God. *"Behold what manner of love the Father has bestowed on us, that we should be called children of God!...Beloved, now we are children of God; and it has not yet been revealed what we shall be, but we know that when He is revealed, we shall be like Him, for we shall see Him as He is"* (1 John 3:1-2).

Your own trying by your own strength isn't the answer. See

chapter two. But if you want the gritty details of how that's accomplished, stick around for the next chapter.

◆◆◆◆◆◆◆◆◆◆◆◆◆◆◆◆◆◆◆◆◆

PRAYING IT OUT

Jesus, thank You for all that You have purchased for me through Your victorious life and resurrection. I am thankful to share in the inheritance of the saints in the light. I want to believe that You have given me rights in Christ, but like the father of the mute boy afflicted with seizures that Jesus healed, I cry "I believe, Lord, help my unbelief." I'm asking You to walk with me and help me to take hold of all that You have given me so that I can honor You with my life.

Fill me with Your Spirit of power so that I can overcome the enemy so that my family and those around me who don't know You can experience Your grace through me. I love You and want to see Your power set me completely free so I can set others free alongside You, as You created me to do. In Jesus' Name, I pray. Amen.

LIVING IT OUT

Do you know your rights? Do you know the things that Jesus has promised to you that you now have available to you for your everyday walk with God? If you can't say right away what you know God has provided to you through the cross, then you need to take a journey in the Scriptures. Ask your heavenly Father to reveal to you what He has provided to you in Christ, and search the Word to get those promises so you can begin to trust in them.

Speak the truth to yourself about them too. When the enemy tells you that you are stuck in sin, tell him that you have freedom in Christ, and *you* now get to choose how you live. You can choose to obey God. You are no longer a slave. You have the power to break free. Now start breaking free and living in freedom. You can set others free!

CHAPTER 6
THE OVERCOMER'S INHERITANCE: POWER TO SUCCEED

"Our old history ends with the cross; our new history begins with the resurrection."
— Watchman Nee

Perhaps you now understand that as a child of God, *you have power*. But you may say, "power to do what?" I'm glad you asked. **You need to know what you can do through Christ.** You know who you are in Christ. You know what you have in Christ. It's time to know what you can *do* through Christ. Let's return to Romans 6 and verse 11. This is the first time in the entire passage that Paul gave a command. He gave us ten verses about identity before finally—based on the truth of all ten verses—presenting a command. So in verse 11, he says, *"...likewise, you also reckon yourselves to be dead indeed to sin."* He says to "reckon yourselves." Now, what does "reckon" mean? It's about belief. In Georgia, where I'm from, it means, "I guess so." Someone asks, "Is your daddy home?" We'd say, "I reckon he is." Well, that's in Georgia. But in Romans 6:11, it means something else! The Greek word for "reckon" is an accounting term. It means to *count* something. It's a mind thing, a belief thing. It's an inside thing, not an outside thing because the inside comes first before the outside shows up.

So he is saying to ***consider*** **yourself as dead to sin. Decide that you are dead to sin.** I can preach it *to you*, but I cannot believe it *for you*—and you can't believe it for me. It could be true all day long, but it'll do you no good until you "reckon" it, until you decide that you really are dead to sin like the Bible says. Reckon yourself *dead* to sin.

Now, how do we do that? One of my all-time favorite authors, Watchman Nee, tells us:

> What, then, is the secret of reckoning? ... If it is a fact that I have fifteen shillings in my pocket, then with great ease and assurance I can enter fifteen shillings in my account-book. God tells us to reckon ourselves dead, not that by the process of reckoning we may become dead, but because we are dead. He never told us to reckon what was not a fact. Having said, then, that revelation leads spontaneously to reckoning. We must not lose sight of the fact that we are presented with a command: "Reckon ye..." There is a definite attitude to be taken. God asks us to do the account; to put down 'I have died' and then to abide by it. Why? Because it is a fact. When the Lord Jesus was on the cross, I was there in Him. Therefore I reckon it to be true. I reckon and declare that I have died in Him. Paul said, "Reckon ye also yourselves to be dead unto sin, but alive unto God [Romans 6:11, KJV]." How is this possible? "In Christ Jesus." Never forget that it is always and only true in Christ. If you look at yourself you will think death is not there, but it is a question of faith not in yourself but in Him. You look to the Lord and know what He has done. 'Lord, I believe in Thee, I reckon upon the fact in Thee.' Stand there all the day.

God help us to reckon!

Reckon what exactly? Ourselves "dead to sin."

DEAD AS A DOORNAIL

What does dead mean? Does it mean sick? Asleep? Under anesthesia? Here is what "dead" means... it looks something like this: If you go down to a local funeral home and there's a funeral going on—we're talking wall-to-wall people, a guy in a casket, the whole deal—imagine you go in there and scream, "Fire!" right there in the middle of the crowded room. My guess is that that place would clear out in about fifteen seconds, but there's one dude that isn't going to move, right? Who? The dead guy. Why? Because he's *dead*. "Dead" means *dead*.

Listen, you don't need some seminary graduate to tell you what dead means; you know what it means. The Bible says, "reckon yourself to be dead," and listen, **the same response that a dead man has to "Fire!" is the same response that every born again child of God ought to have to sin.** We're dead to sin but alive to God in Christ Jesus! Are you daily reckoning yourself as dead to sin—dead to that old life? You can say, "That's not who I am anymore!"

You see it, don't you? There's a *choice* to be made here. That's why God makes "reckon yourself dead" a *command.*

The problem is we let the Devil convince us that what God says is dead isn't dead.

Once, a lady who had been married about 50 years died. So her family hosted a little funeral at a little country church. They sang; the preacher preached, and pallbearers came, picked up the casket with the woman in it, and walked it out down a little winding road out to the grave for the graveside service with her widowed husband walking somberly behind. They got about halfway down that little winding road, and one of those pallbearers accidentally tripped over a rock. Now, they didn't drop the casket, but it was shaken really hard. And whadya know? The shaking revived the lady! (I guess she wasn't as dead as they thought.) Would you know it, she lived three more years—bless her heart—before she died again.

Well, they had a similar little service in that same little church; the same preacher preached; the same people came; the same pallbearers showed up, and there she lay in the same casket. At the end of the funeral, pallbearers picked up the casket and took it out down that same church aisle and down those same steps to that same little winding road with that same husband walking behind them. They made it to about the same area where that pallbearer had tripped over that rock a few years earlier, and the husband was overhead to whisper, "Hey, man, watch out for that rock." In other words, if it's dead, leave it dead!

Your old life may not *feel* dead, but truthfully, sometimes the reason it doesn't feel dead is because we keep taking the wrong roads! We keep tripping over the same rocks! And we know what those "rocks" are, don't we?

So it's not a matter of whether your old life is dead or not. It's a matter of whether you are going to take a different route. Are you going to take a different way and avoid the "world rocks," the "flesh rocks," and the "devil rocks" that keep tripping you up? You have a choice.

See if you can hear the power of choice in Romans 6:12. *"Therefore do not let sin reign in your mortal body, that you should obey it in its lusts."* Did you catch it? You don't have to "let!" In Ephesians 4:22, Paul then says to "put off the old self," which makes it clear that you *can* choose to actually do something about that sinful old self that keeps bothering you. You can "put it off" and "put on" something else in its place. What does that mean? It means that I *don't have to* give in to that old temptation. I *don't have to* repeat those patterns. I *don't have to* fall into those same ditches. I can be an overcomer.

LANGUAGE DETERMINES CULTURE

But here's where our language breaks down. Instead of saying, "*I can,*" we say, "I should." **We have a "should do" mentality instead of a "can do" mentality, and a lot of times, that's what defeats us.** Think of how we talk: "Well, I guess I *should* read my Bible more. Well, I guess I *should* go to church today. Well, I guess I *should* try to witness to the waitress. Well, I guess I *should* be nicer to my wife." Right? Listen, what if God is trying to get us out of "should do" attitudes and get us into "can do" attitudes? Can you see the difference? What would happen in your life if you started talking like this? *"I can* be an overcomer." "I *can* read my Bible and get something out of it." "I *can* share my faith boldly with the waitress." "I *can* love my wife as Christ loved the church." "I can raise my kids in the fear and admonition of the Lord." *"I can* surf the web without looking at what stains my conscience." *"I can* trust God with my tithe"—not I *should*; I *can.* If we did this, what would happen? I know this: too much of church preaching is about "should do," but God is wanting us to operate in "can do." What's the difference? Here it is: "should do" is *law;* "can do" is *grace.* And it's right there in verse 14 of chapter 6: "sin shall not have dominion over you."

In other words, it shall not run your life. Why? Because you're not under "should do," you're under "can do." You're not under law; you're under grace. And **grace isn't license to sin; grace is the ability to overcome sin.**

> ### *"'Sin shall not have dominion over you' means your issues shall not run your life."*

Paul said, *"I can do all things through Christ who strengthens me"* (Philippians 4:13). *"His divine power has given to us all things that pertain to life and godliness"* (2 Peter 1:3)—*all* things. I'm telling you, victory is not just for the preacher or for the grandma who has been saved for 50 years. Victory is not just for somebody who has graduated seminary and knows a bunch of the Bible by heart. *Victory is for every single born again child of God.*

Is it a process? Yes. But here's the process. Over time, we learn and grow, and we begin to really believe in who we are in Christ and what we have in Christ. As we come to believe in that reality, we realize what we can do through Christ. We can daily reckon ourselves as dead to sin but alive to God in Christ Jesus!

God is saying to count yourself dead to sin. Old things have passed away, and behold, all things have become brand new.

Know who you are in Christ.

Know what you have in Christ: freedom, rights, power.

Know what you can do through Christ.

Daily, reckon yourself dead to sin.

And lastly, you need to know how to do it. Know how to count yourself as dead to sin so you can walk in victory.

KEEPING YOUR GLASS FULL IS THE ONLY WAY TO EMPTY IT

In verse 13 of Romans 6, Paul says, "... do not present your members as instruments of unrighteousness ..." What does he mean by "members?" He means "body parts." That's literally what it means. So Paul says, "... *do not present your members (body parts) as instruments of unrighteousness to sin, but present yourselves to God as being alive from the dead, and your members (body parts) as instruments of righteousness to God.*" So what does he mean? **Sin isn't a problem if there are no instruments to play that tune, if there are no body parts available to take that wrong action.** Sooner or later, it's about what you put your hands on, what you set your eyes on, what you entertain with your ears, or where your feet take you. Sin shows up in the body. So he says to take your hands, your eyes, and every other part of you, and stop presenting them as instruments of unrighteousness to sin. Present yourselves to God instead. How do you do that?

> *"Sooner or later, it's about what you put your hands on, what you set your eyes on, and what you entertain with your ears."*

Well, a companion book to Romans is Galatians, and Paul

continues this conversation there. In Galatians 5:16, he says, "... *Walk in the Spirit, and you will not gratify the desires of the flesh.*" So you have to stop walking in the flesh so that you can walk in the Spirit, right? No, that's not what it says. It says to *walk in the Spirit, and the effect is that you will not fulfill the lusts of the flesh.*

See, here's where we get it wrong, and here's why we struggle. We say, "God, I'm going to stop this and stop that, and start this and start that. I'm going to stop presenting my members as instruments of unrighteousness and sin so I can present myself to God." In other words, I'm going to *subtract* so I can *add*. But that is *not* what the Word of God is saying. It's saying to *walk in the Spirit*, and *you won't* fulfill the lust of the flesh. It's telling us to add and the subtraction is taken care of by default of the adding!

I'm telling you, this is a huge paradigm shift for most Christians. The best illustration of this principle that I think I've ever heard comes from the life of D.L. Moody, a great American preacher of yesteryear. He walked in to preach one time before a large congregation, placed an empty glass on the pulpit, and then asked the question, "How do I get the air out of this glass?" Nobody had an answer. Well, can you pour it out? Last time I checked, an upside-down glass is just as full of air as a right-side-up glass. Now, when he asked that question, of course, everybody was whispering to each other, thinking and trying to figure it out. How do you get the air out of that glass? While they struggled to figure out an answer to a seemingly simple problem, here's what Moody did with the glass on the pulpit: *he pulled out a pitcher of water and filled the glass.* Hear me, now. The way to get the air out of the glass is not by focusing on getting the air out of the glass. The way you get the air out of the glass is by focusing on pouring in something else because whatever you pour into the glass automatically, by default, displaces what was previously there.

Can you see it? **If your hands are busy blessing people,**

building the kingdom, and working for the Lord, doing what God wants them to do, those hands don't have time and energy to do what the Devil wants them to do. Feet that are busy following God's lead don't have time to take you where the Devil wants you to go. Tongues that are busy blessing others and encouraging others and talking about Jesus don't have time or energy or room to backbite and gossip and criticize. Friend, what would happen in your marriage if you got a grip on this? What would happen in your workplace? What would happen in your emotional life? What would happen to your future? What would happen if you said, "Oh God, would You fill me so full of You that there's no room for anything else?" That's how you do it.

STAYING ON THE ALTAR

We're called to "present ourselves to God as being alive from the dead and our members as instruments of righteousness." What if we just came to God and said, "God, these are not my hands. They're Your hands. So You do with these hands whatever You want to do with these hands, because they're not my hands. Lord, these feet are Your instruments. They will take me to work to earn a wage and put food on my family's table, but I also want them to take me to work as a missionary because that's what I am. Help them not to take me where I ought not go. Lord, these are not my eyes; these are Your eyes, and as Psalm 101:3 says, 'I will set no unclean thing before my eyes.' You bought and paid for these eyes with Your blood. They're Yours." What would happen if you just told God that your life is not your own because you were bought with a price and everything pertaining to your life belongs to Him?

As someone once said, "The only problem with a living sacrifice is it tends to crawl off the altar." Sometimes we just need to crawl back onto the altar. "Jesus, here is all that I am, and all that I am belongs to You, Jesus. Fill me so full of You there's no room for that old stuff." Hudson Taylor, a great missionary to inland China, said this—"Let us give up our work, our plans, ourselves, our lives, our loved ones, our influence, our all, right into God's hand. And then after we've given all to him, there will be nothing left for us to be troubled about." God is not trying to put you in bondage when you surrender to Him. He is trying to set you free—through surrender—to be the new creature He says you are.

> *"What would happen if you just told God that your life is not your own because you were bought by Him, for Himself and his glory?"*

There's not one person reading this who's saved but yet does not have access to victory. If you are confident you have given your heart to Jesus and He has come to live inside of you, then He has written your name in heaven, and that is a reservation that cannot be canceled. Through Jesus, there is victory and access, *full* access. **The question is: will we believe God? Will we take Him at His word?** Will you say, "Lord, if You say that's who I am in You, then that's who I am in You. I won't argue." Will you tell Him, "Lord, I want to know *what I have* in Jesus. You say I have freedom, and I want to *live* like a free man! You say I have rights. I want to exercise my rights against the enemy! You say I have power. I want to use it daily to reckon myself dead to sin and alive to God in Christ Jesus. You say I'm bought with a price. I'm not my own. So, Lord, I take every part of who I am—from my head to my toes—every part of me where sin tries to show up, and I submit it to You. Lord Jesus, would You show up instead?"

How do you think God's heart would respond to someone who came to Him and said, "Lord, take all that I am and use it in my school and my workplace. Use it in my family and in my relationships. Use it in service and in ministry for Your glory. I don't want to waste my life. Jesus paid it all, and it all belongs to Him." Why don't you become that person today? Go to Him and let Him have your all. He will welcome you and lavish His love on you.

◆◆◆◆◆◆◆◆◆◆◆◆◆◆◆◆◆◆◆◆◆

PRAYING IT OUT

Father, thank You for Your steadfast love for me despite my constant attempts to run my own life. I love You, and I want You to be the Lord of my life in truth—not just in word. I believe You have purchased me by the blood of Your Son, Jesus, and the life I now live I want to live for Him, Who, for my sake, died and was raised.

Fill me to the brim, Holy Spirit, so that my cup really overflows, so that there is nothing left in me but You spilling out of me onto my family and coworkers and friends, onto strangers and others who need to experience Your grace. Take me wherever You want to take me. Use my talents, my professional skills, my money, my time, my spiritual gifts, and magnify Your name. None of it belongs to me anyway. Lord Jesus, put to death that old man that You buried with You in the tomb, and by Your resurrection power, make new life rise up in me so my body can be an instrument of righteousness. Change my world by changing me. In Jesus' Name, I pray. Amen.

LIVING IT OUT

Do you have a "can do" mentality, or are you stuck on "should do?" Watch when you read Scripture this week in the days ahead, and see if you can catch yourself saying what you should be doing.

Then, reframe it on purpose, telling yourself what you can do because of Jesus' finished work for you. Repeat that to yourself all day if you have to. You also want to stay full, so as you consider what you *can* do, begin to do it with every spare minute so that you stay too busy to let your members be used as instruments of unrighteousness. If you ever doubt you're walking in the Spirit, stop and pray. Ask Him to help you do so, and thank Him that He reminded you. If you do give yourself to God, He will use you, but if you find yourself crawling off the altar to do your own will, stop and lay yourself before God to re-surrender. The fact that you do this whenever you do it is the sign of the Spirit's work in your life. It's no accident you are reading this book, and it will be no accident when your victory begins to ramp up like never before!

CHAPTER 7
OVERCOMING IN FINANCES: HIDDEN KEY TO EVERYTHING

*"What we do with our money shows
what we truly believe."*
– Randy Alcorn

*"When we acknowledge God's ownership, every
spending decision becomes a spiritual decision. No
longer do we ask, 'Lord, what do You want me to
do with my money?' The question is restated, 'Lord,
what do You want me to do with Your money?'"*
– Howard Dayton

As you begin to grasp who you are in Christ and what you have in Christ, one of the very first things that should come to the fore-front of your mind—if you're being honest—is money. **If you're genuinely evaluating your life to begin walking by the Spirit and letting Jesus live through you, one of the main things He will start to deal with is what you do with your pocketbook.** Why? Because He wants all of you, and *"where your treasure is, there your heart will be also"* (Matthew 6:21, ESV). The truth is inescapable, and Jesus talks more about money in the Gospels than most other things you might think of, so you know there's a good reason. One is this: there is much overall life victory that comes when you get victory in the area of stewardship.

I heard a story once about traveling circuses. Back in the old days when there was no television or internet, they were a ma-jor form of entertainment. They would roam the country, going town to town, and when they showed up the whole town would shut down, and people would fill up the tents to see these weird, wild, impressive acts. Nearly all of them would have a strong man routine somewhere in the lineup. What he would do is he'd get up on the stage and lift heavy things, bend things, and break things, wowing the crowd with his brute strength.

In one particular circus, there was a renowned strong man who always closed his act the same way. After lifting heavy things, breaking things, and bending things, he would take a raw lemon and ram his finger through the end of the lemon—making a hole. Then, with this powerful arm, he would squeeze out all the juice before issuing a challenge to the crowd. If anyone in the crowd could squeeze just *one more drop* out of that lemon, they'd be granted a $500 reward. (That would be like $5,000 today!) It was a *big* deal, a lot of money. But nobody could ever do it. He was so strong that by the time that lemon left his hand, it was as if there was no juice in it. So the strongman confidently gave that challenge to masses of people all over the country for years and years until finally, he met a rather surprising candidate.

Here's what happened. He did the act as he had always done, closing by grabbing the raw lemon, ramming his finger through the end of it, squeezing out all the juice, and issuing the challenge to the crowd. All of a sudden, peals of laughter began ringing out in the back of the room. A man had stood up to take the challenge, but he was the exact opposite of what anyone would expect. He was not some large, burly young brute. He was a 78-year-old, 110-pound, emaciated-looking little man, and it appeared he was about to embarrass himself. In spite of the laughter of the crowd, he headed to the stage to grab that lemon. The crowd mocked and jeered as loud as they could as he stepped up and took the lemon out of the hand of the strongman. With a look of determination, he hunkered down and squeezed with all his might, ignoring the howling crowd. Several moments passed with the raucous laughter continuing unabated, until finally—the laughing stopped. A hush fell over the crowd as a little crystal of lemon juice began to form on the old man's wrist. It steadily grew until it was large enough that gravity took over, and that droplet of lemon juice fell to the ground.

The place erupted in applause, the crowd gladly offering the fellow a standing ovation. The strong man stood there, dumbfounded, having to go to the safe for the first time in his entire career to fork over $500 to a spindly old man. He couldn't believe it. While he counted out the reward money, he couldn't stop staring at the man, saying, "Listen, I've seen the best try this. I've seen the biggest try this. I've seen the strongest try this! Nobody's ever been able to do what you just did! And look at you! How in the world were you able to pull this off?" As the old man counted his money—with a twinkle in his eye—he replied, "It was easy. You see, I'm the treasurer at the First Baptist Church in town. I do it all the time!"

That funny little story hits at the heart of a resistance that exists for so many of God's people when it comes to finances. For some reason, when a pastor stands up, preaching through the Bible, and he gets to a place there that talks about money or possessions, all of a sudden he feels like he's having to extract drops from dry lemons. **It's just a reality that there is an aversion to giving that has embedded itself in the Body of Christ.** This is all too often the truth, and God wants to do something about that in me and in you. But know this: when we get liberated in this one area, it's like the lock on a safe has spun into place, and "click, click, click," we see unlocked doors to victory and blessing in every area of life.

GOD X-RAYS THE HEART THROUGH THE POCKETBOOK

So let's grab a Bible and turn to Malachi chapter 3. Malachi was the last prophet of the Old Testament, and this was the last thing God had to say to His people before giving them the "silent treatment" for 400 years. The very *next* thing He had to say was "Jesus is here to save the day," (that's the gospels!) and that was after the big break between the Old and New Testaments. If God is about to shut His mouth for 400 years, you better believe the last things He says are going to be pretty strong. So through the prophet Malachi, God addressed a lot of things that were wrong in Israel, and one of the main issues was their stewardship of money & possessions—what they did with their "stuff." Malachi is full of scathing rebukes, but he laid out the case for each grievance very clearly and usually started each section of the book with a question. Malachi 3:8-12 is no different, and that's where we begin:

> *Will a mere mortal rob God? Yet you rob me. "But you ask, 'How are we robbing you?'" "In tithes and offerings. You are under a curse—your whole nation—because you are robbing me. Bring the whole tithe into the storehouse, that there may be food in my house. Test me in this," says the Lord Almighty, "and see if I will not throw open the floodgates of heaven and pour out so much blessing that there will not be room enough to store it. I will prevent pests from devouring your crops, and the vines in your fields will not drop their fruit before it is ripe," says the Lord Almighty. "Then all the nations will call you blessed, for yours will be a delightful land," says the Lord Almighty.*

Three things we notice here.

First, obedience in giving is a *principle* that is *personal* with *God*.

Second, obedience in giving has a *purpose* that is *practical* for the *Church*.

Third, obedience in giving includes a provision that is *promised* to *you*.

Let's unpack each of these one by one.

OBEDIENCE IN *GIVING* IS A PRINCIPLE THAT IS PERSONAL WITH GOD

First of all, notice that obedience in giving is a principle that is personal with God. What any man or woman gives or doesn't give is between them and God alone. Look at Malachi 3:8, "will a man rob—*the pastor*?" Nope, not what it says. "Will a man rob—*the church*?" Nope, not what it says. It says, "Will a man rob *God*?" I want to be crystal clear here. When we don't give, we're not robbing the church or the pastor, we are robbing God Almighty.

God is a giver! "For God so loved the world that He...*gave*," and what did He give? A nice little tip? Some chump change for a beggar? Leftovers? **No, He bankrupted heaven itself and gave the blood of His only Son so that we could be saved and born again. God is a *gracious giver*.**

Hey, you know what? *Satan* is a taker. God's Word says that the "thief" comes only to "steal, kill, and destroy" (John 10:10). So, that means that when I decide I'm not going to tithe or give, I am aligning myself more with Satan the taker than God the giver. I don't know about you, but I want to be like God.

So God says that when we don't tithe, we rob *Him*. Now the last time I checked, the Bible said we have freely received, and so we are to freely give. To whom much is given, much is required. Knowing what we've received in Christ, how can we not *freely* give?

God says in the passage that He has been robbed in tithes and offerings. Let's talk about definitions. What does He mean by tithe? The Hebrew word for tithe literally means "tenth." This means that if you earn $500 per week, the tithe is $50. In other words, $50 of the $500 doesn't belong to you. It belongs to King Jesus. If you buy a house and sell it a few years later for a profit of $50,000, then $5,000 of the $50,000 doesn't belong to the power company, the new car dealership, or in your wallet for your next vacation. It belongs to Jesus; that is the tithe. That's the 10%. If you buy some stock on the stock market, then you sell the stock a few years later for $25,000 more than you paid for what you had, then $2,500 is the tithe. That tithe is *not* your money. It is God's money.

God said you've robbed me because you have not been tithing. Now, I know what some people will say here: "Brother Scott, we're not under the law anymore." You're right, but guess what? Abraham tithed 700 years before the law was given, and Jacob tithed 400 years before the law was given. In fact, Jesus endorsed the tithe in Matthew Chapter 23. Why? *Because the tithe is not tied to the law. It is tied to God's ownership of everything.*

For the believer, possession does not equal ownership. Maybe you missed that. Let me say it again. For the believer, *possession* does not equal *ownership*. **You might possess it, but He owns it all.** As 1 Corinthians 4:7 says, "... *what do you have that you did not receive?*" You received it from God, which means you don't own it.

> ## "For the believer, possession does not equal ownership."

Have you heard about the church that needed more parking space? They ran out of parking space, and the store across the street was closed on Sunday, so its parking lot was empty. Somebody in the church went to the store owner and asked if they could park there on Sundays. The owner said, "You may use my lot for Sunday parking on one condition. You can park there every Sunday except one Sunday each year. For one Sunday a year, on a Sunday of my own choosing, I'm going to chain it off. You can't park on it that day." The church member was surprised. "You're saying we can park in your parking lot, but just one random Sunday every year you are going to chain it off? Why in the world would you do that?" The owner winked, "Because I don't want you folks to forget who owns the parking lot."

You see, we have to be reminded, don't we? We start acting like it's our money because we think we earned it. Do you know what the Bible says in Deuteronomy 8:18? It says "... *remember the Lord your God, for it is He who gives you power to get wealth.*" So what does that mean? That means it's His money—not my money. **The only reason you can get out of bed in the morning, the only reason you can put one foot in front of the other and go to work to earn a wage at all, is that God, by His grace, has given you one more day to do it.** He's the source. He owns it all, and He ropes off 10% because we need to be reminded that He owns 100%.

So God speaks in Malachi about the people robbing Him in both tithes *and* offerings. What's the difference?

The offering is above the tithe. The tithe is the first 10% of what God provides to us, and the offering comes out of the remaining 90%.

The tithe is directly proportional to your income. The offering, on the other hand, is in proportion to your generosity.

The tithe is essentially a debt you owe, whereas the offering is a seed you sow.

The tithe goes to the storehouse, the offering goes to wherever God directs you to give it.

The tithe says, "God, You own it all." The offering says, "Thank You for letting me enjoy it on the way."

Now, by the time we get to chapter three of Malachi, God is ticked off; God is offended—because, in "tithes and in offerings," He has been *robbed*!

HAVE YOU EVER BEEN ROBBED?

Have you, personally, ever been robbed? I was 12 years old. We lived way out in the sticks on a chicken farm. We lived so far out, you had to head toward town to go hunting. My dad had gone on to be with Jesus but every Wednesday night, my younger brother, my mom, and I would get in the car, and we'd drive one mile to our church. So one particular night we pulled out of our driveway to head to Wednesday night church. As soon as we came out of the driveway, somebody immediately started riding our tail the whole way. It was one of those jacked-up, four-by-four deer hunting trucks, and they put their bright headlights on our back glass and just rode us all the way. Well, as soon as we got to the church and pulled into the driveway, they whipped that truck around fast. They went the other way at about 70 miles per hour on the country road we had just turned off of. It was odd, but we didn't think much about it past that. We were just glad to be safe at church.

It turns out that some thieves had been scoping out the community, watching everybody's routine. We were next on their target list, and they knew that we went to church every Wednesday night and knew we were always occupied for about two hours. They had also made sure that all three of us who lived in the house were in the vehicle so they could be sure the house would be empty. So these folks watched us go to church, then went back and robbed us. When we got home, there were clothes and boxes strewn all over the carport; inside there were drawers pulled out of their sockets; the refrigerator doors were standing open, and our little poodle was having cardiac arrest! We'd been robbed! That was what I told everyone for years at least.

> *"The tithe is essentially a debt you owe,*
> *whereas the offering is a seed you sow."*

Eventually, however, I was corrected in telling the story. A law enforcement officer listened one time, and he said, "Stop telling that story that way, Scott. You were not robbed." Now I know he was an officer of the law, but I was indignant hearing that. I defended myself, "I *was* robbed. I was there. That's what happened." He wasn't put off in the slightest. He said it again: "You were not robbed, Scott. You were *burglarized*." Um, what?

What's the difference?! Well, wouldn't you know, there's a difference! Burglary is what happened to us, not robbery. Burglary is when somebody sneaks around behind your back, knowing you're not looking and glad you're not there. And they're hoping they don't get caught. That's what happened to us. However, robbery is different. Robbery is when you are walking down the street, minding your own business, and somebody comes up to you and puts a gun or a knife in your ribs, opens up their other hand, and says, "I want you to take whatever valuables you have on you and hand them over to me." They are watching you. They know you're watching them. And they don't care. Robbery is eyeball-to-eyeball, gutsy, confrontational theft.

When God got down to this business of not tithing and giving, He didn't say, "You've been withholding behind my back, sneaking around about it." What He said is more like you walking up to God on the street, putting your fist in His ribs, and saying "God, I know You know I'm doing this, and I'm going to do it anyway. I'm going to take what I know belongs to You, and I'm going to spend it on myself." Well, it's no wonder that God is upset! No wonder "it's personal!"

By the way, it's no wonder that God is upset with so much of the Western church today. God told His people that they were cursed with a curse—the whole nation of them—because they had robbed Him. I know Jesus breaks every curse, but sometimes we work under a *functional curse* of our own choosing because we're not obeying God's principles in an area of our thought life, our temperament, our words, our sexuality, or whatever. This applies to finances too.

Here is the statistic: One of the largest evangelical denominations reported that 85% of their members do not tithe. So 85% of them know what the Word of God says, yet are telling Him, "Thank You, but I would rather spend that 10% on myself," more greedy than godly.

You don't have to guess about it either. Ask some church folk to give, and they grunt when they get their wallet out, then by the time they pull that one-dollar bill that they're going to give, George Washington goes blind because it's been so long since he's seen the light!

WHAT CAN YOU AFFORD?

You may tell me, "Brother Scott, we can't afford to tithe. We're so poor that when the church has communion, our whole family sneaks back down for seconds." Or, "Brother Scott, we can't afford to tithe. We're so broke that American Express called us up and told to us leave home without it." Or, "Brother Scott, we can't afford to tithe. We're so broke, our baloney has no first name!"

What's amazing is that so many say, "I can't afford to tithe," but can afford to make their car payment. They can afford to pay their light bill. They can afford to rent a movie, or go out to eat, or go on vacation. Hmm, can't afford to tithe, but they're still putting money in their 401(k), SEP, and IRA.

When you or I say, "I can't afford to tithe," here is what we are *really* saying: *"I'd rather steal 10% from God and trust in that 10% to meet my needs rather than giving God His 10% and trusting in God to meet my needs."*

Ouch.

One report said that the average evangelical Christian gives 2%—not 10%—to the local church. Now wait a minute. Guess how much Uncle Sam gets at tax time from the average evangelical Christian? About 31%. Now, I want you to really think about this. **We praise God, and we complain about the government, but God gets 2% while the government gets 31%.** The fact is, God won't put you in jail if you don't tithe, so you take your chances with Him while toeing the line with Uncle Sam. Listen, if the average Christian treated the IRS the way they treat God, 80% of them would be in jail right now!

Ouch, again.

I'm going to give you an illustration. It's not original to me. God used it. It's in Malachi 1:8. He said, "Try giving to your governor what you've been giving Me." They'd been giving Him sick sheep and leftover lambs and the worst of their flocks for sacrifice. God said, "Try it! Give it to your governor, and see if he'll take it. I've been more patient with what you've been giving Me than your government would." Friend, I'm telling you, we *have* to get our priorities back in order. Listen, I believe that the government has a role. Don't misunderstand me, but understand God. We *owe* God what's His. He said it all belongs to Him, and He asked for 10%. In 1 Samuel 2:30 God says, "those who honor Me I will honor, and those who despise Me shall be lightly esteemed." This is a principle that gets *personal* with God.

OBEDIENCE IN GIVING HAS A PURPOSE THAT IS PRACTICAL FOR THE CHURCH

So Malachi establishes that obedience in giving is personal with God, but it also shows us that obedience in giving is practical for the church. Go to verse 10, where it says, "bring all the tithes into the storehouse that there may be food in my house." The "storehouse?"

The storehouse was a part of the temple complex used for the storing of the grain, goods, and gold that were brought in as tithes from God's people. It fed the full-time priests, and it fed all the widows and orphans.

Now what is the modern day storehouse? I believe it is the *local church.* Your tithe goes to the storehouse, and the storehouse is the local church where your talents are employed and where your fellowship is enjoyed. It's the place where your family is spiritually and corporately fed as well as spiritually and corporately led. That's the storehouse.

I'll tell you what the storehouse, the recipient of the tithe, is not. It's *not* the TV preacher. It's *not* the para-church organization or other ministry. Thank God for Cru, thank God for Samaritan's Purse, thank God for all those great ministries—to them go some offerings, but not the tithe. The tithe goes to the storehouse.

Our ministry depends on the financial gifts of God's people and has since 1996. But I've always been clear about this when I've said: "Don't give your tithe to our ministry. The tithe goes to your church. Offerings are appreciated and used in our ministry, but the tithe belongs to where you plug into the local body of believers."

God's local church is the primary arm of ministry. So we go now to the practical purpose of bringing that tithe into your church. God says, "bring the whole tithe into the storehouse *that there may be food in my house.*" How do you think the church lights stay on? "Well, there's a little switch in the back you just flip." No, you know somebody has to pay that bill or that switch doesn't work. Right? Who pays for that small group curriculum we all learn from? Who pays for the salary of the pastors and staff who are leading and ministering? Who funds all those ministries in your church that are reaching out to the community? How does all of it happen? You get what I'm saying. It doesn't happen without God's people—that's you and me—bringing in our tithes to the church.

God says, "the whole tithe." In other words, everybody ought to tithe and everybody ought to tithe the *whole* tithe. That's a full 10%. Your tithe may not be the same amount as my tithe, but if you're sitting on a pew, and you're not tithing, but your mom or your brother or Ms. Jones is tithing, then somebody else is footing the bill on the pew you're sitting on, so-to-speak. Should that be okay? Not at all.

There's something inside of you, and there's something inside of me that reminds us it is wrong not to do our part. So *everybody* ought to tithe the *whole* tithe. What does that mean? That means never less than 10%. If you earn $50 per week, and you give God $4, you're still robbing God by $1. Don't hold back! Why, don't hold back? Because if you're holding back in that area, you're holding back somewhere else. This is not really a money issue. This is a heart issue. I didn't say that—Jesus said that. Jesus said, "where a man's treasure is, there his heart is also." It's not a wallet issue, it's a heart issue.

> *"This is not really a money issue.*
> *This is a heart issue."*

You might say, "Can I start with 2% and work my way up to 10%?" A lot of people preach that and teach that, to just start where you are and work your way up. The problem is, "working your way up" usually doesn't happen. And think about it. What if we applied that logic to everything regarding obedience? How would that go?

As an example, let's say next Sunday your pastor is up preaching church and somebody gets saved. A man comes down the aisle and gives his heart to Jesus. Your pastor walks down and kneels beside him to pray with him. Then your pastor says, "I'm so glad you're our brother in Jesus now. You're born again! Praise God! Is there anything else we can pray for you about?" The guy looks at your pastor and says, "Well, I have one problem I need some help with." Your pastor asks, "What problem?" The guy explains, "For the last two years, I've been cheating on my wife with five other women. What do I do about that?" Your pastor looks back at him and says simply, "Oh, don't worry about it. Just wean yourself off the ladies by one per month until you're a one-woman man again, faithful to your wife." (Insert laugh emoji here, right?!) That just won't fly!

You see, Mama was right when she taught us that "partial obedience is disobedience." Yes, giving tithes and offerings is rooted in obedience which is rooted in trusting God. But like anything else, God challenges us to "go all the way with it" and really put Him to the test on His Word. In doing so, He's working to set us free, just like with every other principle this very book talks about.

HAPPY = TRUST AND OBEY

There's a song we used to sing growing up that went like this:

Trust and obey,

For there's no other way,

To be happy in Jesus,

But to trust and obey.

Usually, if the light of "happiness in Jesus" isn't filling our soul, it's because our trust switch or our obedience switch is flipped off.

Proverbs 3:9 says to "honor the Lord with all your possessions and the first fruits of your increase." Would he command us to tithe off our gross income and not deliver gross on His promises? (I don't want "net" blessings, I want "gross!") God will always honor His Word.

Now, I will add one more thought: The fact is that many times some can't give the 10% because they're not managing the other 90% right. So you might have to put a little Dave Ramsey in there and get your budget together to learn to steward as well as you can. But I'm telling you, if you give to God, if you do what He says,

He will take care of you and everything that pertains to you. God is more than big enough to make the 90% go as far as it needs to go. And as you watch Him do that, your faith will grow to believe His Kingdom principles about every other area of your life.

◆◆◆◆◆◆◆◆◆◆◆◆◆◆◆◆◆◆◆◆◆◆◆

PRAYING IT OUT

Holy Father, we are thankful that Your mercy is new every morning, especially when we have been disobedient with what You have entrusted to us. Thank You, Lord Jesus, for paying the debt I owe on the cross. Because I have received freely, please flood my heart with generosity so that I can cheerfully give back to You, not only the full tithe but even offerings out of the overflow of my gratitude to You. Change me so that I can experience the abundant life You have promised if I will walk with You in obedience.

I am sorry that I have so often robbed You, and I repent. I turn from that path and choose to give You all that I am and all that I have. Please also use my obedience to fill Your storehouse so that Your name is honored through the ministry of Your church. God, give me the faith to give You what is Yours, to sow beyond even that into the needs I see around me. Help me, also to steward past the tithe to the remaining 90% of what I have been given so that I can honor You and see You come through. In Jesus' Name, I pray. Amen!

Do you tithe? Do you ever give offerings to God out of the generosity of your heart beyond the tithe? Be honest about this, and then have an honest conversation with God asking Him to reveal to you *why* that is, whether your answer was yes or no. God does not see as man sees. He looks at the heart. If the answer was "no" to either question, God understands your weakness, and He is able to sympathize with it because Jesus was tempted as we are. However, He also has a standard, and He is calling you to account in regard to that standard. Will you yield to Him today? Confess to Him how you have been robbing Him, and really begin to evaluate what you spend your money on each month. Re-do your budget, and right off the top, first thing, remove 10% for God to use as He sees fit. It belongs to Him. Then finish the budget and ask God to provide for all the rest because you are trusting His promise.

CHAPTER 8
OVERCOMING IN FINANCES: EXPECTING MIRACLES

"Earn all you can, save all you can, give all you can."
– John Wesley

"I never would have been able to tithe the first million dollars I ever made if I had not tithed my first salary, which was $1.50 per week."
– John D. Rockefeller

Now, you may have heard all of this about giving God the tenth no matter what, no matter how much you have, and you might be saying to yourself, "Look, Brother, I hear you, but there are 100 pennies in a dollar, and 2 + 2 = 4. I know the math; I know what's coming in and what's going out, and I can't afford to tithe."

Hey, I hear you. And I sympathize with your hesitation. But allow me to remind you that we serve the Jesus who supernaturally multiplied a boy's fish-and-chips to feed over 5,000 people in one sitting. We serve the Jesus who called a dead Lazarus out of a grave. We serve the God who used ravens to feed Elijah on the backside of a desert. **If He can do those things, then He can take care of His people when they trust Him.**

Obedience in giving is not only a principle that is personal with God, it has a purpose that is practical for the church.

OBEDIENCE IN GIVING HAS A PURPOSE THAT IS PRACTICAL FOR THE CHURCH

What are the implications of your tithing and my tithing for the Body of Christ, the Church? Let's do some math. Let's take an un-named church I once preached at where 80% of the members were not tithing, and 20% were, which is average for most churches in the United States. I checked, and that church regularly received $25,000 in income per week. You might say, "Hey, that sounds like enough money," but that's not the point. The gauge is God's gauge, not our gauge. And God's gauge says 100% of His people who have an income tithing a full 10%. Now, let's say $20,000 of the $25,000 was coming from the faithful, full-tithing 20% members, and the other $5,000 was coming from the miscellaneous folks who are giving somewhere between 0 and 10%. Consider this: what if that church started fresh next week, and everyone took God at His word, saying, "I'm going to look at my gross pay for this pay period, and I'm going to give my full tithe. I'm going to write a check for 10% of the whole." What would happen?

By the way, do you tithe off the gross income, or do you tithe off the net income? Let me answer with another question: do you want to get blessed off the gross, or get blessed off the net? I think you want the gross!

So how much would we have next week if this church had every member give their allotted tenth? We wouldn't have $25,000. The church in question wouldn't even have $50,000. Nope, keep bidding up. They would have over $100,000 per week in income! Can you imagine $100,000 per week coming into a church that was accustomed to seeing "only" $25,000? And the thing is, I'm not even talking about free will offerings, I'm just talking about tithing.

I once shared this principle in a sermon at a church of about 300 people who together were giving $3,000 per week. I said,

"Listen, Folks, if I have my numbers right for what everyone together could contribute with a full tithe, we ought to see $15,000 per week starting next week." Guess what? The next week we missed it—we had $14,740—but it was close, right?! And here's the kicker: month after month the total stayed high. In fact, it was during a spiritual renewal conference that I gave that challenge, and there was a large contingency from the church down the road, and *their* church saw total giving *double* the next week from just the few families who had attended that particular service!

WHAT CAN GOD DO WITH OUR COMPLETE TRUST CONCERNING STEWARDSHIP?

Think about it. What could happen if we would just tithe? Do you understand? You can build a house of worship in Uganda for only $1,000. We have Ugandan brothers and sisters who are standing in fields Sunday after Sunday, sometimes in the rain, worshiping God. Imagine! Your church can build them a simple church building for about a thousand dollars! Hey, with all God's children tithing, your church could build a structure on the foreign mission field every single week and never even miss the money! Wow! You think God would bless that?

Let me ask you a thought-provoking question you may have not considered. If you had multiplied thousands more per week coming in, do you think word would get out in your community that something was happening? Do you think it would impact your witness in the community as a church?

How about growth? Do you think you could afford as many staff as you need? Do you think you could build buildings, or extend existing ministries, or send kids to camp for free (kids who might get saved as a result)? Can you imagine being able to go to a local school and say to all the kids, "I want you to go to camp with our church this summer, and it won't cost you a dime." They'd have no excuse not to go hear the Gospel, and *you'd never even miss the money*. Can you imagine?

> ## *"God never put you in a position to decide what should be done with His money."*

You know what else? If God's people started tithing, we could say "bye bye" to bake sales, barbecues, and car washes. (Hallelujah! Not a day too soon!) Think about it. **Every time the Church of the Living God has to go out into the community and pedal our wares to raise money to do what God said to do anyway, it is a sad indictment on the unfaithful 80% who aren't obeying God.** "Bring *all* the tithes," He said!

Someone reading this (certainly not you) might be saying, *"Well, I'll tell you what. I'll tithe—but I'm going to designate my check to my favorite ministry because I don't like the finance team, and I don't like the pastor. I'll bypass the general fund and put it where I want it to go."* What this person needs to understand is that God never put us in a position to decide what should be done with His money. God is big enough to handle your finance team. God is big enough to handle your staff. God is big enough to handle any decision-maker in your church. Your job is to be faithful, and God will reward you on the other side.

Someone says, "Well, since I don't like the church leaders, I won't tithe at all! That'll show 'em!" Again, God never put us in a position to decide what should be done with His money. Our job is to trust and obey. As a matter of fact, if we are faithful in giving, and the leaders of the church mismanage it, you better believe that God Himself will show them what's up. They'll learn the easy way or the hard way; He'll make sure. He takes what's His seriously.

But don't miss it, and I hope you see it: tithing and giving have practical purposes for the church.

OBEDIENCE IN GIVING INCLUDES A PROVISION THAT IS PROMISED TO YOU

Not only is obedience in giving a principle that is personal with God, and not only does it have a purpose that is practical for the church, obedience in giving also includes *a provision that is promised to you.*

If you look at Malachi 3:10, the middle of the verse says, "... try me and test me now in this." This is *the only time* in the whole Bible that God ever looks to His people and says, "Test me," and it has to do with money and possessions.

Do you know what He's saying? He's saying, "Jump. See if I'll catch you. Go out on a limb. See if I'm out there." It's right there: *"'Test me now in this,' says the Lord of hosts, 'see if I will not open for you the windows of Heaven and pour out for you such blessing that you will not have room enough to receive it.'"*

In case you think that's just Old Testament, take a look at Luke 6:38. Jesus said, *"Give, and it will be given to you."* Then, just in case there's some confusion, He clarified how it would come to you: *"...good measure, pressed down, shaken together, and running over will be put into your bosom. For with the same measure that you use, it will be measured back to you."* Here's the bottom line. Don't ever forget this. **You cannot outgive the greatest Giver there ever has been and ever will be—God himself. You. Can't. Outgive. God.**

My mother taught me to tithe, and I tithed all my life. Every time I made money, I tithed. However, I would always calculate that tithe down to the last penny, like $55.06, for example. But the offering part, that over-and-above-the-tithe part, well... that was something I still needed to learn.

It was my wife Scarlet who actually taught me about giving. She has a genuinely generous heart. After we'd only been married a couple of weeks, she said to me one day, "Scott, God has put it on my heart to give away about half of my closet, a bunch of dress clothes and such." I was thinking the stuff just didn't fit anymore, but she assured me they were items that still fit. So then I figured it must be the stuff that maybe had gone out of style. She said, "No, no it's in style." Then she went on, "God just convicted me. I really have more than I need. There are some women in my life who could really use these, and I just want to bless them with it." Hey, sometimes it's not money, it's stuff. (We are living in the storage unit generation, are we not? By the way, will we not stand before God regarding what we did with things of value that we paid money to store that we weren't going to touch for 10 years when we could've been doing kingdom work with it? Just a thought!)

So my wife was about to start giving away clothes, and I was like, "Honey, we just got married, and we're in ministry. I was counting on some of those clothes lasting at least ten years, y'know." She just replied, "Honey, I'm telling you, I've got plenty." So she was giving away and giving away. Let me tell you what happened. It wasn't two weeks into giving away her extra clothes that, one morning, we heard a knock on the door of our hotel room in Lexington, Tennessee where I was preaching at the First Baptist Church there. At the door stood the youth minister's wife. She said, "Is Scarlet here?" So I asked Scarlet to come to the door. The youth minister's wife looked at my bride and said, "Scarlet, I was praying this morning, and it's almost like I heard the Lord so clearly say to me that I'm to take you shopping and buy you two brand new outfits today. Do you mind? Can we go shopping together?" So she took my wife out shopping and bought two new outfits! My wife is pretty conservative in her tastes, so one of those outfits really did last about 10 years. (It was made completely out of rubber. Kidding!)

My generous wife eventually got into gift baskets. Do you remember when gift baskets were a big thing? Do you know what I'm talking about? These were wicker baskets full of girly, good-smelling stuff that women really like, all wrapped in cellophane with a big ribbon. Scarlet loved to give gift baskets. She would put together gift baskets, and we would we go to minister at a conference somewhere, pull up in the motor home, and meet the pastor's wife. "Here's a gift basket." She might even give away a couple to church members, perhaps, if she heard that in that church someone was going through a hard time or something. Deacon Chairman's wife, "Here's a basket." Kid's Ministry Director, "Here's a basket." Then we'd get in the motor home after ministering at that church where she gave away two or three baskets, drive three states away, pull into the next parking lot of the church where we were scheduled to minister, and there'd be like, three, four, or five ladies standing out there with baskets for my wife! This was some crazy math—giveaway two, get five back? It got so bad, there were so many baskets coming in, that I couldn't even hardly drive the motorhome with baskets all jammed in behind me. My wife says, "What are we going to do with all these baskets?" I said, "Well, we ain't gonna give them away! I can't breathe here!"

YOU CAN'T OUTGIVE THE GIVER

Jesus said, "Give and it shall be given to you, pressed down, shaken together, and running over." This means you cannot outgive God. Here's what I've learned: God keeps His promises. What He said was clearly, "Go tithe and give, and see if I don't open the windows of heaven for you and pour out for you such blessing there won't even be room enough to receive it." He even went on to say in Malachi 3:11, *"And I will rebuke the devourer for your sakes, so that he will not destroy the fruit of your ground, nor shall the vine fail to bear fruit for you in the field."* **That's their source of income, and God is promising that it will continue to**

come in. God even goes so far as to say, *"All nations will call you blessed, for you will be a delightful land."* He's saying that when there's a recession, people are going to look at your life and say, "What is going on? Why are they still so 'taken care of?'"

When God said, "I'll rebuke the devourer," I believe I've seen this happen. Tires lasting longer, washing machines not breaking down as much, and your income not being frittered away on constant medical expenses. You may say, "You're crazy, Man. God doesn't do that." Well, He did that in the Old Testament. God's people spent 40 years wandering in the wilderness, and they never even had to make a new pair of shoes. God made their *shoes* last. You think God can't do that with everything else in your life? Do you wonder why every time the bucket fills up, it drains out? There's a hole in it! Why? We're not tithing. We're not giving. We're not doing what God said.

Let me be clear here that I understand the exceptions. There can still be times of reversals financially in spite of tithing. But I believe these are rare and usually for a much bigger goal of God in your life and mine to teach us something deep and lasting. But often, not surprisingly, finances are often later restored in abundance.

> *"Do you wonder why every time your bucket fills up, it drains out? There's a hole in it. We aren't giving like God said."*

It's important to keep the giving mindset. God said, "I'll open the windows of heaven for you and pour out for you such blessing you will not have room enough to receive it." Now, why would an all-wise, all-knowing God give so much blessing to His people that they don't even have a place to put it? Because He knows they don't plan to store it up anyhow. You see, God is giving back to givers, and do you know what givers like to do? They like to give.

Now you may be saying, "You sound like one of those name

it and claim it preachers. You're sounding like one of those prosperity guys who say we give in order to get." No, if that's what you take away, then you have missed the point. Listen, we don't give in order to get. We give to get... to get to give!

SPONGES VS. FUNNELS

Listen, God doesn't bless sponges. He blesses funnels. Last time I checked, when you send water through a funnel, that funnel gets soaking wet. God wants to send blessing *to* your life so He can send blessing *through* your life, turning you into a blessing for others while you get the blessing all along the way. He's into *channels*, not *reservoirs*. You can't outgive God.

It reminds me of a story. One time a pastor had everybody stand for the offering. He said, "I want you to reach over and take out your neighbor's wallet. Now give like you always wanted to give." What am I saying? I'm saying you *can* give like that. Why? Because it's God's wallet. Your wallet is *God's* wallet.

This is real life stuff. I *can't even tell you* the number of times people have told me what great things happened when they started tithing.

Once, a lady called me and said, "Scott, we'd been waiting for two years on an insurance settlement. I started tithing that week, and that very week the settlement check showed up in the mailbox."

Another lady, a retired pastor's wife who had opened a restaurant with her husband in retirement, came to me and said, "Scott, we've been trying to sell our restaurant, but it hasn't worked out. We haven't been able to sell it in our little town. After I heard you preach on stewardship, I knew I had to tithe and I certainly wanted to. I was going to write my tithe check for the month for $450, but if the check went through for my tithe, it would overdraw my account by $450 according to my paper check register." (She was old school and made the entries by hand.) She continued, "Scott, the very next week my bank statement arrived in the mail, and I reconciled my check register with the bank statement. Looking at it, I immediately realized there was an error *in my favor*."

I said, "That's amazing!"

She said, "No, that's not the surprising part. What's amazing is that the error in my favor was for exactly $450!"

I remember this one fellow in Norfolk, Virginia where I preached on stewardship Sunday. The guy started tithing that night, Sunday night. Then, that Wednesday, the last night of the meeting in which I was preaching, he came to me and said, "Scott, you will not believe this. My boss walked in today out of the blue and gave me a raise."

I said, "Charlie, that is great, Man! That is awesome."

He said, "No, that ain't the best part. The raise is a *10%* raise— the exact amount of my tithe!"

You ready? I got more!

Another time long ago I was preaching on the subject of stewardship at a church in the middle of Georgia, and I touched on the subject of giving. I kept noticing a young couple in their 30s kept passing notes down to each other on the third row. I didn't know if they were paying attention or not, but when I gave the invitation, they came down to the altar and stayed there, crying, holding each other for a while. After the service was over, I was in the pastor's office with the pastor when his phone rang. He answered, "Yeah, he's right here," then handed the phone to me. It was that couple.

The husband said to me, "Scott, we're new believers. We'd never even heard of this tithing thing. But we decided when we got home we were going to do it. So we wrote our check and put it in an envelope because we were going to mail it tomorrow so we wouldn't spend it before Sunday. While my wife was licking the envelope, I noticed the light was flashing on the answering machine. So, I hit the play button. A guy had left a voicemail while we were at church tonight, a guy who we had been waiting to hear from for two weeks. He said, 'Jeff, I've changed my mind. I do want to buy that horse after all that you're selling. If you still got it, I could be at your house in the morning with a check for $1,200.'"

Now, I am not saying that this will solve all your problems, but I am saying that God will keep His promise. I believe that when you begin to step out in faith, you'll find God meets you there every time and does things that only He could do and that only could be explained as His faithful intervention.

Why is this important? Because if you just get this right, you'll see how big God is, what lengths He'll go to in order to bless you and your faith, and thereby every other area of life will experience an increase as a result. This is a simple choice you have to make and then watch God work. I'm telling you, miracle after miracle after miracle happens. Why? Because there's a principle at work here that's personal with God.

When you're not tithing and giving, you're robbing God. When you start tithing and giving, you stop robbing God. Start tithing and giving, and watch what happens. Obedience in giving includes a provision that is promised to you. **You can't outgive God.**

✦✦✦✦✦✦✦✦✦✦✦✦✦✦✦✦✦✦✦✦

PRAYING IT OUT

Father God, I praise You for what You're doing and what You've done. You're a big God. You're bigger than my problems. You're bigger than the gaps in my finances, and You own all of it. So

Lord, today I want to be found faithful. Today, I want to be responsive to You. Lord, if You can't trust me with green, dirty paper, how are You going to trust me with souls and influence and success and advancement? So, Lord, I want to be "faithful in the little things" so You can make me "ruler over many things."

Turn me from a sponge into a funnel, and flow that blessing through me. I want my own stories of Your provision! Lord, expand my faith, and may You receive all the praise and the honor for it. Lord, make me and my church greater than we have ever been through obedience. Help us trust You so that I can see You move like never before and accomplish more than has ever been done. In Jesus' Name, I pray. Amen.

LIVING IT OUT

When you give, are you reluctant? To gain a truly generous heart, meditate on all that God has done for you and given to you. Do this each day, especially before each financial decision and whenever God provides you with new income. Remember that when you face the decision to give, you can *never* outgive the Giver. He gave us life, breath, and everything, and it all belongs to Him. Begin to remind yourself that it all belongs to Him. We are not our own anymore but have been bought with a price. Refuse to let yourself think like an owner and instead maintain thinking like a steward.

Ask God when He wants you to give next, how much, and to whom. He may surprise you, but you just need to step out in faith and give even if you are not confident that money will be replaced, because God will reward the step of faith. He promises that He will, right here in this passage from Malachi. He will then pour out heaven's riches in answer to your need and to your church's needs as you and others become faithful. Just imagine what could be done for the kingdom of God with all that blessing!

CHAPTER 9

THE OVERCOMER'S SECRET WEAPON: LEARNING YOUR WEAPON

"Enemy-occupied territory—that is what this world is.
Christianity is the story of how the rightful king has
landed, you might say landed in disguise, and is calling
us all to take part in a great campaign of sabotage."
— C.S. Lewis, "Mere Christianity"

We're on a quest to live the overcoming Christian life, and God has not sent us on this quest without tools in our toolbelt to handle whatever challenges we may face. In fact, we have some significant weapons at our disposal as we wage war against the enemies of our souls: against Satan, his minions, our own fleshly nature, and the fallen world in which we live.

Let me just say from the outset, that I believe we're in the last days. I know not everybody believes that. But if we're living in the last days, I believe the Devil is pulling out all the stops because he knows his time is short. This is not game time, and he isn't playing games. **I believe we need to be using every single weapon God gave us as born again children of God.** And I'm going to give you here one of the most powerful weapons that a believer could ever use, but it's one of the most rarely used weapons by believers.

You can almost call it a "secret weapon." It's not secret to the Devil. He knows about it because his tail has been stung many times by it. But most *believers* don't see this as a weapon. So we live in defeat, in discouragement, and in confusion because we're not using this weapon. And I'm telling you, if we'd use this weapon, it'd change everything.

Now, I don't know what kind of application you're going to have for this weapon because it could be different for different people. For some of you, it's going to be a personal application to handle your circumstances. You're going through tough times right now where you need to be using this weapon because your faith is hanging by a thread. I get that. You're weary. There's some stuff out of control in your life, and so God is going to make a very personal application for you.

For others, the Holy Spirit is going to make applications for what's going on culturally in our nation and our world, and I believe there are some serious applications for this particular weapon in that arena. By the end of it all, I pray that God is glorified and that you're encouraged and equipped in a way that really could make a difference.

The weapon that I want to reveal to you—one of the most rarely used weapons in the believer's arsenal—is the weapon known as "praise."

IN THE PRESENCE OF MY ENEMIES

To lay some foundation for this weapon and its appropriate use, we're looking at 2 Chronicles 20. Let me give you the background: You have the kingdom of Israel—of God's people—split in half. There's a northern kingdom and a southern kingdom. The southern kingdom of Judah is led by King Jehoshaphat—yes, that was his name. Bless his heart. In the chapter here, Jehoshaphat had three armies coming against him, and the armies of Judah were definitely the minority party. He felt overwhelmed and overpowered. Have you ever felt like that? I want you to watch what unfolds now.

It happened after this that the people of Moab with other people of Ammon and others with them beside the Ammonites, came to battle against Jehoshaphat. Then some came and told Jehoshaphat, saying, "A great multitude is coming against you from beyond the sea, from Syria; they were in Hazazon Tamar, (which is En Gedi)." And Jehoshaphat feared, and set himself to seek the Lord, and proclaimed a fast throughout all Judah. So Judah gathered together to ask help from the Lord, and from all the cities of Judah they came to seek the Lord.

Then Jehoshaphat stood in the assembly of Judah and Jerusalem, in the house of the Lord, before the new court, and said, "Oh Lord God of our fathers, are You not God in heaven, do You not rule over all the kingdoms of the nations, and in Your hand is there not a power and might, so that no one is able to withstand You? Are You not our God, who drove out the inhabitants of this land before Your people Israel, and gave it to the descendants of Abraham Your friend forever? And they dwell in it, and have built You a sanctuary in it for Your name saying, 'If a disaster comes upon us—sword, pestilence, or famine—we will stand before this temple and in Your presence and cry out to You in our affliction, and You will hear and save.'

And now, here are the people of Ammon, Moab, and Mount Seir— whom You would not let Israel invade when they came out of the land of Egypt, where they turned from them and did not destroy them—here they are, rewarding us by coming to throw us out of Your possession, which You've given us to inherit. O our God, will You not judge them? **For we have no power against this great multitude that is coming against us; nor do we know what to do. But our eyes are upon You."**

Now all Judah, with their little ones, their wives, and their children stood before the Lord. Then the spirit of the Lord came upon Jahaziel the son of Zechariah, the son of Benaiah, the son of Jeiel, etc. And then he said, "Listen, all you of Judah and you inhabitants of Jerusalem, and you Jehoshaphat! Thus says the Lord to you: 'Do not be afraid or dismayed because of this great multitude, for the battle is not yours, but God's. Tomorrow go down against them. They will surely come up against the Ascent of Ziz, and you'll find them at the end of the brook before the Wilderness of Jeruel.

You will not need to fight in this battle. Position yourselves,

stand still, and see the salvation of the Lord, who is with you. O Judah and Jerusalem!' Do not fear or be dismayed; tomorrow go out against them, for the Lord is with you.' "Now watch this." Jehoshaphat bowed his head with his face to the ground, and all Judah and all the inhabitants of Jerusalem bowed before the Lord, worshiping the Lord.

Skip down to verse 21.

When he had consulted with the people, he appointed those who should sing to the Lord, and who should praise the beauty of his holiness, as they went out before the army and were saying…

And here's the chorus: *"Praise the Lord, for his mercy endures forever."*

Say that aloud, wherever you are. *Praise the Lord, for His mercy endures forever!* One more time. *Praise the Lord, for His mercy endures forever!*

Now, watch what happens next in this story…

When they began to sing and to praise, the Lord set ambushes against the people of Ammon, Moab and Mount Seir, who had come against Judah; and they were defeated. For the people of Ammon and Moab stood up against the inhabitants of Mount Seir to utterly kill and destroy them. And when they had made an end inhabitants of Seir, they helped to destroy one another. So when Judah came to a place overlooking the wilderness, they looked toward the multitude; and there were their dead bodies, fallen on the earth. No one had escaped. When Jehoshaphat and his people came to take away their spoil, they found among them an abundance of valuables on the dead bodies, and precious jewelry, which they stripped off for themselves, more than they could carry away; and they were three days gathering the spoil because there was so much.

My grandma used to cook something called "cat head biscuits." I'll tell you what, those cat head biscuits were *amazing*. She lived across from our little chicken farm, and I could walk right across from there. As soon as I'd hit the door, man, the smell would hit my nostrils, and I'd be in caloric heaven. You open those things fresh, steam just pouring out, and throw butter at it—butter melts before it even hits the bread. It's unbelievable. I'd say, "Mamaw, how in the world do you make these cat head biscuits? My mom can't make them this good." And with a twinkle in her eye, she'd say, "I made them from scratch."

Sometimes, it would be "fried apple pies"—nothing pie-like, just cooked sweet apple mash folded up in a buttery shell of crust. Other times, it would be pound cake, crispy on the outside, soft in the middle. Every time I would ask her, "How in the world do you make [fill in the blank]? My mom can't make it this good," with a twinkle in her eye, she'd respond back to me, "I made them from scratch."

One day, I went home and said, "Mama, listen, I've got the secret to make you cook better. If you can ever get a can of that 'scratch' stuff, you can make anything you wanna make, and it'll be awesome on top of that!"

I want to teach you about the weapon of praise, and I want to *start from scratch*. As a matter of fact, I'll teach this concept for you in two parts and, therefore, two chapters. The first part is **what praise is**. You can't use praise for what it does if you don't understand what praise is. So we're going to talk about what praise is. And then we're going to talk about **what it does**. Some of that comes from our story. Some of it's out of the Scriptures, so just bear with me. Let's go. What is praise?

PRAISE IS PROCLAMATION

Truth number one is that praise is a form of proclamation. You see in the Psalms—the hymnbook of Israel—that praise was conducted in the context of a great assembly. Why? Because something was being proclaimed. In Psalm 26:6-7 (NIV) it says, *"I go about your altar, O Lord, proclaiming aloud, proclaiming aloud your praise, and telling of all your wonderful deeds."*

Now, think about this. First of all, every praise song we sing is either **to** God or **about** God. Either way, it always contains one of two things: truth about **who God is** or **what God has done**. Think about it. Whether we're singing a song to God like *I Love You Lord* or one about Him, such as *Because He Lives*, we're proclaiming **who He is** and **what He's done** in praise.

Naturally, therefore, praise always involves the lips at some point. The Bible says in Hebrews 13:15, *"Therefore by Him let us continually offer the sacrifice of praise to God, that is, the fruit of our lips, giving thanks to His name."* I know somebody will say to this, "Well, I'm kind of introverted. I just want to praise the Lord in my heart." Hey, I understand you can praise the Lord in your heart, and usually, that is where it starts. However, according to the word of God, praise is "telling" of all His wonderful deeds. If praise is really happening inside your heart, sooner or later, it's going to find its way out of your mouth!

Jesus said, "Out of the fullness of the heart, the mouth speaks." So, praise is a form of proclamation.

PRAISE IS PUBLIC

The second truth about praise is it's public.

Consider these scriptures:

Psalm 33:3 *"Sing to Him a new song; play skillfully with a shout of joy."*

Psalm 47:1 *"Oh, clap your hands, all you peoples! Shout to God with the voice of triumph!"*

Psalm 66:1 *"Make a joyful shout to God, all the earth!"*

Psalm 81:1 *"Sing aloud to God our strength. Make a joyful shout to the God of Jacob!"*

Psalm 98:4-6 *"Shout joyfully to the Lord, all the earth; break forth in song, rejoice, and sing praises. Sing to the Lord with the harp, with the harp and the sound of a psalm, with trumpets and the sound of a horn. Shout joyfully before the Lord, the King."*

Psalm 71:23 *"My lips shall greatly rejoice when I sing to You, and my soul, which You have redeemed."*

Please be aware: **If God says something even one time, it's a big deal. But if God repeats himself, you had better pay attention.** He didn't say "Shout unto me" just once or even just twice. God said, "When you get together to worship me, I want to hear you shout," and He clearly places emphasis on it!

Do you know why I believe that the average churchgoer thinks it's more exciting to go to a football game on Saturday than a church gathering on Sunday? It's because the average churchgoer hasn't learned yet how to biblically praise the Lord. Sometimes, I wonder if part of the reason that the culture thinks God is dead is perhaps because the average church in the average community acts like they're having a funeral for Him every Sunday! I'm telling you, God is alive! Let's act like it!

> ### *"God said, 'When you get together to worship me, I want to hear you shout.'"*

One time, a lady came to a pastor and said, "Pastor, you know, I'm really not liking what's going on at church."

The pastor said, "Can you explain?"

She replied, "Well, people are getting way too loud and crazy during the worship service on Sundays."

He tried to clarify, "What do you mean exactly?"

She looked surprised. "Do you not hear them? They're clapping during the music. Some of them are raising their hands. That's never been done in our church until you came. Certain times while you're preaching, they'll holler, 'Amen,' 'Praise the Lord,' or 'Hallelujah' while you're preaching the sermon."

The pastor nodded his head. "Yes, ma'am. I understand that. And you said there's a problem?"

She said, "I looked in my Bible, and nowhere do you ever see Jesus clapping His hands. Nowhere do you see Jesus raising His hands, or hollering 'Amen' or shouting 'Hallelujah.' Nowhere do you see Jesus doing those things. What do you have to say to that, Pastor?"

He wasn't phased. "Well, Ma'am, you know what, you're right. I've been studying the Bible a long time, and you're right. Jesus never clapped His hands, raised His hands, or shouted, 'Hallelujah,' as far as we can tell by the Gospels. But Ma'am, have you ever noticed that everybody He touched did *all* those things?"

I've been touched. How about you?

Maybe you say, "Sure, but I think we are to be more dignified than that in church." Well, who said so? Let me ask you a question. You're a human being, so what do you get excited about?

Some may say "Oh, I get excited when an overinflated pig skin gets carried past a white chalk line on Saturday by an overgrown, hairy, sweaty boy wearing Styrofoam and plastic." Ok, so let me get this straight: You get excited over a touchdown that nobody is going to remember two weeks from now? And that same person thinks: "So what is there to be excited about in church? Why should we be shouting and celebrating in church?" Hmmm, maybe this? I was lost, but now I'm found! I was on my way to hell, and now I'm on my way to heaven! I was alienated from God, and now He's my Father, all paid for by Jesus!

So, praise is public. That's why it gets musical. You see Psalms like Psalm 150, saying, *"They praise the Lord with the sound of the trumpet. Harp and lyre, tambourine and dancing, string and flute. Clash of cymbals, resounding cymbals."* By the way, that's a reference to drums. I still don't understand why some (only a few left) have problems with drums being used in worship. The next time I'm in some church, and someone comes up to me and says, "I don't think we ought to have drums in the sanctuary," I'm going to suggest she write Psalm 150 on the chalkboard a hundred times! I believe if you can play the drums well and you're saved, you ought to be doing it in church. It's wrong for the honky-tonk downtown to have more use for a talented drummer than the church of the Living God when God is the One who gifted them with the talent!

PRAISE IS PHYSICAL

Take a look at verses 18 and 19 in our passage from Chronicles. They "bowed down to worship. They stood up to praise." It notes their physical posture. So, we see that praise is also *physical*. Listen to the physicality of worship in these verses:

Psalm 47:1 *"Clap your hands all you nations; shout to God with cries of joy."*

Psalm 30:11 *"You turn my wailing into dancing."*

Psalm 149:3 *"Let them praise his name with dancing."*

Psalm 63:4 *"I will praise you as long as I live, and in your name I will lift up my hands."*

Psalm 134:2 *"Lift up your hands in the sanctuary and praise the Lord."*

Now, if it makes you feel any better, I can tell you that the Hebrew word for "dancing" really just means...wait for it...dancing! It all sounds exciting, doesn't it?

Somebody says, "Well, preacher, that's the Old Testament." Take a gander at 1 Timothy 2:8: "I *command men everywhere to lift up holy hands in prayer.*"

Wow. Is that the New Testament? Listen to his language. I **command men everywhere** to lift up holy hands. When's the last time you walked into the church, a prayer meeting was going on, it was filled with believers, and they had their hands raised? Right there, he says to lift up holy hands and pray. "Well, that's for other types of churches." Really, is it? It isn't Pentecostal, Baptist, Methodist, Presbyterian, or Greek Orthodox. It's **Bible**. Physical expressions of praise, like the raising of hands, are not a denominational assignment. They supersede denominational lines. There is a "why" behind the action. And the "why" is what we need to understand.

Specifically, let's look at the lifting of the hands. Do you understand that the lifting of the hands carries a universal meaning with it? **The exposure of the palm has always been a sign of surrender.** That's why you see it in certain salutes. For instance, in Nazi Germany, they said, "Heil Hitler," and when they said that, how would they salute? They would expose their palms upon the pronouncement of their allegiance to Hitler. In other words, when the Nazi German army would say, "Heil Hitler," they were saying, "We surrender to no one but Hitler." Now, the U.S. military salutes how? Palms down. Why? Because the U.S. military surrenders to no one.

The Bible says to lift up holy hands. When we come into worship and we begin to praise God, we lift up our hands. What we're doing is we're sending a message to every angel, demon, and human looking on that we surrender to no one but Jesus!

The fourth truth about praise is that it is *proactive*. That means it's never passive. Nobody can do your praising for you, any more than they can eat your three meals per day or get your education for you. You choose to do it, or you don't choose to do it, but it's not passive.

By the way, proactive means it's rooted in *choice,* not *feeling.* Many of us don't praise the Lord, don't clap our hands or sing or raise our hands in the times we don't *feel* like it, literally *because* we don't feel like it. We might even assume that if we praise the Lord when we don't feel like it, we are doing something hypocritical. But think about it: God *commands* praise. One cannot command an emotion. I can't say to you, "Feel sad," and you start crying. It doesn't work like that. But I can say, "Stand up" and "Sit down," "Open the book," "Close the book," or "Turn the knob." I can tell you to *do* something. God commands praise because praise isn't rooted in a feeling; it's rooted in a choice. It's not rooted in emotion. It's rooted in volition. God commands praise because it's something we need to choose to do. It's not about how you and I feel.

> *"Praise isn't rooted in a feeling; it's rooted in a choice. It's not rooted in emotion. It's rooted in volition."*

Here's what I've noticed: we keep waiting on emotion to lead our actions, but **if we wait on emotion to lead our actions, we won't obey God most of the time.** What I have found in every area of life is that you just have to obey God, whether you feel like it or not. If God said, "Praise," just start praising! Decide to do it. And when you decide to do it, that looks like something in the real world. You're going to clap your hands. You're going to start singing to Him. You're proclaiming who He is and what

He's done. You shout unto God, you raise your hand, and you begin to praise Him. And then, here is what naturally happens. In a few minutes, your "feeler" starts to catch up with your "do-er," and you begin to "feel like" what you've been doing for the last few minutes! Actions lead emotions, not the other way around. If you and I just take the time to make the choice, this can happen. Praise is proactive.

PRAISE IS PRE-REJOICING

Another major truth about praise is that it is pre-rejoicing for something coming. **Praise is rejoicing now because we know there's a victory on its way, even though it may not have arrived yet.** You see this all through the scriptures. I could give a lot of examples. One example of this is when Joshua fought the battle of Jericho. They marched around the city once daily for six days, then seven times on the seventh day, before finally stopping at the end and giving a great shout. Let me ask you a question. Did they shout *before* the wall fell or *after* the wall fell? They shouted before the wall fell! Why? Because God had promised them *that the wall would fall*. And so they gave what was in that time a victory signal by shouting, knowing the victory was about to happen because they had a promise.

Be assured of this: no matter how bad it looks in the headlines, no matter how bad your circumstances, and no matter how bad it looks on your social media profile, God's Word is the final word. And the fact of the matter is, one day, every "wall" is going to come down, so we can shout now! We can praise Him *now*, no matter what. God's Word tells us that one day, every knee will bow, and every tongue will confess that Jesus Christ is Lord. Every wall is going to come down; the victory is on its way. Like Joshua and his army, we can go ahead and shout, no matter the walls that stand before us!

◆◆◆◆◆◆◆◆◆◆◆◆◆◆◆◆◆◆◆◆◆◆

PRAYING IT OUT

Father, I come to You in need of a spirit of praise. You are good, and all Your ways are good, and You deserve praise from my lips every minute of every day. My spirit is willing, but my flesh is weak. Too often, I moan, groan, and complain when things happen, even though You have not changed. Guide me in Your Word to really understand praise and grow in me a desire to use it all the time, both in and out of church times. Father, make my life a praise anthem to You, the one who forgave me, redeemed me, and called me Your own. In Jesus' Name, I pray. Amen.

LIVING IT OUT

If you are challenged by the truth in this chapter, especially if you consider yourself withdrawn or introverted, really explore the Scriptures regarding praise, speaking to God and asking Him to change your heart on the subject. Don't leave Him alone about it until you begin to see "the joy of your salvation" restored and increased and escaping from your lips more often. Take opportunities to give God credit in conversations when you're sharing what's been happening in your week with someone else. Say aloud to God how great you think He is when you're driving in your car, and remind yourself of what He has done. Aim to become a child of God who proclaims the grace of your Father aloud at every opportunity.

CHAPTER 10
THE OVERCOMER'S SECRET WEAPON: DEFEATING THE ENEMY

"A mighty fortress is our God,
a bulwark never failing;
our helper He, amid the flood
of mortal ills prevailing."
– From the hymn, "A Might Fortress
is Our God" by Martin Luther

As we discover how to wield the "secret weapon" of praise, perhaps one of the most important attributes that we need to remember is its *power*. Praise is powerful! So what can it do? That's the question. **What does praise do?** Let's draw from the passage in 2 Chronicles 20.

Remember, Jehoshaphat had three armies coming at him, and he went to praise God and to pray to God. The Lord then told him what to do. Jehoshaphat appointed singers and praisers to go out in front of the army. As they began to sing and praise, confusion broke out among their enemies, and they literally destroyed each other without even touching the Israelites. Then the Israelites received the victory and all the spoils.

What does praise do? The first thing to remember praise can do is that it puts the situation into perspective.

Allow me to make a parenthetical statement before we go further. What I'm wanting to get across in these chapters about praise is not really about praise *in church* so much. It's about praise *out there on the other side of the church walls.* What do I mean? I'm talking about using praise as a weapon on the battlefield of faith.

Last time I checked, most of my battles aren't taking place in church on Sunday mornings. Most of my battles are on the other side of that church exit sign. Most of the battles are out there on Monday, Tuesday, Wednesday, Thursday, Friday, and Saturday more than on a Sunday. I'm talking about using praise as a weapon *in the time of attack*, and what happens in church on Sunday morning is only the overflow of that.

> *"Using praise as a weapon isn't primarily about what happens on Sunday mornings in church."*

So when Satan comes to attack—whether it's personal, national, or anywhere in between—you need to put the situation into perspective. And that's what praise does. You'll even find that in Jesus' model prayer. Jesus teaches us how to pray. When His disciples asked how to pray, He gave them what they asked for by modeling a prayer that starts with praise. In Matthew 6:9-13 where this prayer is recorded, Jesus begins, "Our Father who's in heaven, hallowed be your name." He is saying, "Holy is Your name, God," and that's praise. That's proclaiming God's character like we talked about in the previous chapter when defining praise. The Psalms are chock full of praise, and if you take any of the letters in the New Testament, the first chapter is usually a doxology filled with praise for God's character and deeds. **It always starts with praise.** Why? Because no matter the issue, no matter the problem, and no matter the circumstance, praise puts the situation in perspective.

I remember hearing a story one time about a lady who was driving a car and began to drift towards the right side of the road too far. As soon as she went off the side of the road on the right side, she whipped it back hard to the left to correct her mistake. And then she went off the side of the road over there. Then she whipped it back, hard to the right, and she went off the side over there again. This continued for maybe a minute, and she couldn't seem to figure out how to fix her mistake. Well, a cop saw her and thought she was likely driving drunk, so he pulled her over.

He knocked on her window. "Ma'am, what's wrong with you? Have you had too much to drink?" The lady replied, "No, Officer, I don't even drink. There was a tree in front of me, so I swerved to miss it, but there was a tree over there, so I swerved to miss that one, but then there was a tree over there, so I swerved to miss that, and it just wouldn't stop!" The officer simply said, "Lady, that's not a tree. That's the air freshener hanging from your rearview mirror."

She didn't have perspective, did she?

Listen, some of us are driving our lives like that. You're just going from reaction to reaction to reaction to crisis to crisis to crisis as if it all depends on you. You're living as if God is some doddering old man in a celestial nursing home who can't do what He used to do. And I'm telling you, we have to put the situation into perspective. To make the point, that's exactly what Jehoshaphat did in our passage.

When they told him that three armies a whole lot bigger than his were coming to kick him out of his land, what did he do? The Bible says that he "went in to pray." And it tells us the content of his prayer in ve**rses 6-12** of 2 Chronicles. What you'll find is that he was really turning that prayer closet into a praise closet. What was the first thing he did? With three armies coming at him, you might imagine his prayer was basically, "HELP!" Not at all. Listen to what he said: "You are the God of our fathers. You are the God of heaven. You rule over all the kingdoms of the nations. All power and might are in Your hand." He goes in, and the *first* thing he does—before he even petitions for help—is praise God for who He is and for what He's done. Now, why did he do that? Let me ask you a question.

Does God need our praise? Let me ask you this way: is God *more* God if we praise Him? Is God *less* God if we don't? God doesn't need our praise. Jehoshaphat got really, really bad news. It looked dire for the home team. He had an issue. He knew to run to God, and he did. And he began to praise God. Listen, Jehoshaphat was not praising God because *God* needed to hear it. Jehoshaphat was praising God because *Jehoshaphat* needed to hear it. In the face of his bad circumstances, he praised God for who He is, for what He's done, and for what He's promised, and he acknowledged in faith that all the power and might of the nations against him were really in the hand of God. Also, in case you forgot, God still rules over all the nations today.

"The LORD has established his throne in heaven, and his kingdom rules over all." Psalms 103:19

I'm telling you, praise puts our situation into perspective. **Jehoshaphat went into that prayer closet with a problem that was bigger than he was. He came out of that praise closet reminded that God is bigger than his problem.**

The problem is, we think our biggest, baddest, and best is going to scare the Devil. I've had pastors tell me, "Brother Scott, when you come back and preach your next revival, by then, we'll be in our new building. *That's* where we'll make hell back on up. When we get that new big building, we'll get a lot of people saved." Let me tell you something. Satan is not scared of your big building. Maybe we have a 30 pound family Bible sitting on our dresser, and we say, "Look at that Bible, Devil. You're toast!" Listen, that does not scare the Devil a bit, especially if you don't read it. Our biggest, baddest, and best doesn't scare the Devil.

But God has ordained *praise* as a weapon.

> *"The times we need to praise God the most are the times we praise Him the least."*

The times we *need* to praise God the most are the times we praise Him the least. The times we're most discouraged, the times we're most under attack, and the times we're most depressed are when we're praising Him the least when we need to praise Him the most. Listen, how can loneliness stand against you when you're praising God that He promised never to leave us nor forsake us? How can guilt from the past stand when we're praising God that our forgiveness is complete and that there's no condemnation for those in Jesus? How can intimidation from the enemy stand when God has said that we're more than conquerors in Christ Jesus? And if we praise God that when we submit to Him and resist the Devil, He has promised the Devil must flee, then how can the Devil stand? Put the situation into perspective.

AMBUSHING THE ENEMY

Not only does praise put the situation into perspective, **praise also puts Satan in a predicament**. Look at verse 21 of 2 Chronicles. Here's their battle plan. "When the king had consulted with the people, he appointed those who should sing to the Lord and who should praise the beauty of His holiness as they went out before the army..." Imagine being there with his men. "King Jehoshaphat, what's the battle plan? We're ready." He replies, "Well, we're going to take the army and put them out front." They're nodding away. "Right, right, and...?" The king continues, "And then we're going to take the choir and put them in front of *those* guys, between the army and the enemy." You know, folks thought he'd lost his mind!

Do you know what? They used that plan. Why? **Because it was a plan that gave men the least amount of glory and gave God the most.** They understood what the Bible was talking about when it said, *"The weapons of our warfare are not carnal but mighty in God for pulling down strongholds"* (2 Corinthians 10:4). Listen, that hasn't changed today. Our weapons are not through politics. Our weapons are not through machinations, gimmicks, and systems. Our weapons are mighty through God to the pulling down of strongholds.

> *"God spoke, God's people praised,*
> *and the battle was won."*

Listen, God can do whatever He likes and more quickly than we think is possible. One time, a Russian cosmonaut went into outer space and said, "I looked around while I was up there, and there isn't a God. Hear me: No God!" And one day God looked down at Russia and said, "No communism!" and that ripple was felt throughout the entire globe. God can change the whole thing. He can break down the Berlin wall in a day if He wants. He's done it before, and He can do it again. Listen. He's not intimidated by *any* of this stuff. "It's not by might nor by power but by my spirit," says the Lord.

So in our story, 2 Chronicles 20:22 tells us that when they began to sing and to praise, the Lord set ambushes against the people of Ammon, Moab, and Mount Seir. And they were defeated. God's people praised, God spoke, and the battle was done.

SATAN'S ACHILLES HEEL

Now, I want to go a little deeper. God has ordained praise as a weapon. Why? Well, let's talk about it. Think about the Devil a second. Who is he? The Bible gives him a lot of names: Satan, Lucifer, Beelzebul, an angel of light. Let me give you another one. The Bible says he is the prince of the power of the air (Ephesians 2:2). That's an odd-sounding title. Well, God has put Satan on a leash, and it's a long leash, but He's put him on a leash. He's relegated him to a certain turf, and the turf is that which is between the bottom layer of the upper stratosphere and the topsoil on this earth.

He's the prince of the powers of *the air*. That's where Satan hangs out.

By the way, he's interested in the air inside the church as much as the air outside the church. The reality is Satan goes to church more than you do. Every time your faithful pastor proclaims the Word of God from the pulpit and scatters the seed, Satan is like a bird of prey sitting in the rafters, waiting to swoop down and steal that seed before it takes root in your heart and bears fruit. Every time church is on, Satan is there. Satan is the prince of the power of the air.

Now, let's talk about God and how He interacts with praise. The Bible says God inhabits the praises of His people. He makes praise His dwelling place. Psalm 22 verse 3 says, "Lord, you have enthroned yourself upon the praises of Israel." What is Scripture telling us? **When God's people praise, God shows up. Praise invokes the presence of God into a place.**

When we begin to praise, what are we doing? We're singing *into the air*. We're clapping *into the air*. We're making a joyful noise *into the air*. He tells us to raise our hands, where? *Into the air*. And God manifests Himself there. So Satan operates in the air since he's prince of that space, but when we begin to sing praise, we lift up God *into the air*. God inhabits that praise. Praise is the way you introduce God onto the Devil's turf.

So yes, praise God at the red light when you're under attack with discouragement; praise Him when you get out of bed in the morning and Satan is on you like white on rice; praise Him when bad things happen at work and you just want to quit; and when you want to complain instead of pray, just choose to praise, and God will show up.

> *"Praise is the way you introduce*
> *God onto the Devil's turf."*

Hang on, and I'm going to go a little deeper.

The word "clap." The Hebrew word for clap is the word "lis'pok" and means "to strike." To clap unto the Lord is to, at the same time, "strike at" the enemy!

How about this frequent admonishment to "blow the trumpet?" What's going on there? It's the word "taka" which describes the action of blowing a shofar.

In warfare, the sound of the shofar or trumpet served several functions:

1. Rallying Troops: The trumpet sound was used to gather or rally troops for battle.
2. Signaling Movements: It was employed to signal different maneuvers or actions during combat.
3. Intimidation: The loud blast could be used to intimidate the enemy.
4. Announcing Victory: After a battle, it might be used to declare victory.

When we create that music with our hearts, mouths, or instruments, we are, in essence, "blowing our trumpet" in the face of the enemy. Now, is it getting clearer? One powerful purpose for which God made praise is for warfare!

Let's go further.

There's another word for praise, the word "magnify." You've heard this before, as we might sometimes use it interchangeably with praise. Psalms 34:3 says, *"O magnify the Lord with me, and let us exalt His name together."* But there's a difference. Praise means one thing, and magnify means something else.

I remember one time when I was growing up on our little chicken farm. I was about five years old, and I was in the kitchen rummaging around in the "junk drawer." You know that drawer, right? It was full of things like pliers with a missing screw, some bailing wire, some matches that had been half burned, loose bolts of various sizes, a half pad of sticky notes, and a couple of broken pens. You know. The Junk Drawer! So I dug around until I found a little round piece of glass that was thick in the middle and narrow on the edges. It was amazing because when I moved it across objects, it made them appear to be bigger than they actually were. I was blown away! It was like magic! That was the day I began my magnifying career. As a five-year-old, I'd get my magnifying glass and just go around to the cat and the Bible and the clock and this and that, magnifying everything.

Now, I thought I'd reached the pinnacle; I thought it was awesome. I was fine with the potential I'd discovered, but I had no idea just how much it could do until one day, I took my magnifying glass outside—on a *sunny day.* It wasn't long—before I knew—I had—The Power! I took my magnification experience to a whole new level! Now, there were three objects involved in my upgraded magnification process. First, there was the *instrument* of magnification, the magnifying glass. Second, there was the *object* to be magnified, which was the sun. And, lastly, there was a *target*—usually an insect that needed to die! How did this system work? I would focus the white-hot power of that sun down into one little point on that insect, and the power of the sun would do great damage to it.

"When we magnify the Son, Jesus, all the white-hot power of God's presence is concentrated on the backside of the Devil, and there is no escape."

Listen, we're still in the magnifying business. In our praise, we magnify the Lord. We still have three things: the *instrument* of magnification, the *object*, and the *target*. Now, for us, the instrument is our *praise*. Do you know what "praise" means? Listen to this. **The word praise is tehillah, meaning "to cause to shine."** Are you seeing what God put together here? The instrument of magnification is our praise; the object of magnification is the Son, not the S-U-N but the S-O-N, and the target is the enemy. The target is the backside of every demon that has been assigned to you that day. I'm telling you, when we praise, we begin to cause heaven to light up; when we cause, in a sense, the Lord to shine, when we brag on the SON, lifting up Jesus, all the white-hot power of God's presence is concentrated on the backside of the Devil, and there is no escape for your demonic foes!

So at the end of 2 Chronicles 20, in verse 24, it says of Israel's enemies that "not one of them had escaped." Let me tell you something. The Devil can handle your intellect. Do you know why? Because he's smarter than you. You cannot out-argue the Devil. The Devil can handle your emotions; he'll never be afraid of a human rant. The Devil can handle your psychological reasoning; he'll out-analyze you because he's more insightful into human behavior than you are, even your own. He's been studying human nature for centuries. A Safari guide in Africa was asked by a reporter, "Is it true that the animals won't harm you if you carry a torch?" The Safari guide said, "It depends on how fast you carry it." Hey, you cannot outrun the Devil; he's faster than you. You need other options because you're running out of 'em. Here's an idea: go with what God has ordained as a weapon!

God has ordained praise. Praise is what the Devil can't stand. You may say, "I thought the sword of the Spirit is our named offensive weapon, and that is the word of God." Yes, that's true. But I'm not contradicting that here. What do you think is the content of praise? Without the Word, you've got no content for your praise. **Praise is how you take the "Sword" out of the**

sheath and put it into the air where it belongs, where the Devil hangs out.

PRAISE PUTS THE SPOILS (OF WAR) INTO OUR POSSESSION

Let's look at the text one more time in 2 Chronicles 20:24-25:

So when Judah came to a place overlooking the wilderness, they looked toward the multitude; and there were their dead bodies, fallen on the earth. No one had escaped. When Jehoshaphat and his people came to take away their spoil, they found among them an abundance of valuables on the dead bodies, and precious jewelry, which they stripped off for themselves, more than they could carry away; and they were three days gathering the spoil because there was so much.

We see the third truth about praise: that praise puts the spoils in our possession. After praising God and seeing Him defeat their enemies, it looks like Israel stripped off a bunch of their jewelry, Gucci bags, and pinstriped suits and drove a couple of Mercedes home. I like that kind of story.

Now, you might be worrying a little, thinking, "Scott, are you telling me that putting the spoils in our possession is about name-it-and-claim-it? Are you implying a materialistic prosperity promise is in this story?" I'm not saying that at all. As a matter of fact, the promises of the New Testament are a bit different than the promises of the old, which dealt a lot with physical land and property within a physical kingdom God was building. In the New Testament, we're taking territory for the spirit kingdom. I want you to understand that when I'm talking about taking the spoils back and putting them in our possession, I'm talking about **snatching from the thieving hand of the Devil what God intended for you.**

I'm saying God didn't intend for your marriage to be lost and become another statistic. God didn't intend for your kids to grow up in your house and your church only to become prodigals later. God didn't intend for you to put your head on your pillow at night with a tainted conscience because you've been diving into sin all day as a born again child of God. God intended you to have a beautiful marriage that pictures His relationship with the church. God intended that you raise up children who become part of the army of God. God intended you to put your head on your pillow at night with a clean conscience, knowing that your testimony is intact and that tomorrow is another day to serve Jesus! Those kinds of things are what God intends you to have! Satan has been robbing all that from us in the church of the Living God for far too long!

How many broken hearts does your pastor have to counsel? How many overwhelmed parents does he have to listen to who can't keep it together? The kids are going at it again. There's another addiction, another divorce, another church split, and another this and another that. How many times do pastors have to sit down and take time away from equipping the saints, away from leading the church, and away from advancing the kingdom of God on earth? It's all because Satan has just mucked up another marriage or another minister or another testimony, and God never intended it to be the case.

God intends for you to have a lot more victory by using God's weapons. But we don't use them. You don't. Why? Because we're embarrassed. Honestly, I'm talking about me. I need this message my own self. I've dealt with discouragement this week. And I'll probably face it next week, too. I'm sharing this message as much for me as for you.

But I'm going to tell you that if anybody has been exemplary in this, it's my wife. I've seen the enemy attack her with depression and with confusion in times when she was really vulnerable. I've seen her use the weapon of praise in public places even. I've seen her in the grocery store against the backdrop of some really rough stuff going on in her life. I can barely explain all that the Devil was bringing against her. And I've watched her get down on her knees in the produce department with her hands in the air and tears running down her face. People were walking by her probably thinking, "Is that woman crazy?" But she knew that the only hope for deliverance was a *song of deliverance in the time of attack* from the enemy. Are you getting this? The key is that she cared more about getting victory than looking good in front of strangers who don't even know her.

Do you understand? This is the heart of our problem. The reason we haven't seen more victory as The Church is that we haven't gotten to the point where our "desperation factor" exceeds our "embarrassment factor."

> *"The reason we haven't seen revival in the church is we haven't gotten to the point where our desperation factor exceeds our embarrassment factor."*

We worship, sing, do what we do, and obey at the limited level we obey based on what people think of us. And Satan loves it. That's why he's got you in over your head. I'm telling you, once you get to the place where you say, "You know what? I want the spoils. I want the victory more than I want the approval of people. I'm going to do what God says. I'm going to use my weapons. I may look like an idiot. People may write me off as a fool, but I'm going to believe God; I'm going to stand still and see the salvation of the Lord. I'm going to do what He said to do. I'm going to praise Him and watch Him win again in my life. I'm going to do it no matter what anybody thinks." *That* is when you'll start to see the spoils put into your possession.

God has ordained praise, and I've been kicked around long

enough. How about you? **If God has said that praise is the way you make the Devil pay, then I want to make him pay.**

I heard a story one time about a little grandma who lived in Tucson, Arizona. She loved Jesus. She was a widow woman whose husband had died years ago. They let the widows live in a little house in a little row of shotgun houses that all those mill workers used to occupy. Her husband had died long ago, and there she was, living by herself, as poor as dirt, but she loved Jesus. Every morning, she would walk out onto her front porch, put her hands in the air, and say, "Praise the Lord! Glory to God! Thank You, Jesus, for another day!" The cupboard was just about empty; her clothes were threadbare, but I tell you, she was praising Jesus no matter what.

Well, her neighbor who lived in the little house right next door—about four feet from her house—hated it. She was an atheist and didn't believe in God. So sometimes, when this little grandma was out there praising Jesus, she stuck her head out the window and said, "Shut up and go back to bed! Shut up! You're bothering me. There isn't anybody up there. No one is listening to you. Nobody can hear you but me, and I don't want to hear it." This neighbor lady just let that widow have it. But do you know what? She praised God every morning at the same time and in the same way, undeterred.

One day, her neighbor was going to teach her a lesson. Knowing the lady was dirt poor, she went out and bought three bags of groceries and put them on the front porch. The next morning, the poor grandma went out to praise the Lord—and she bumped into those groceries. She looked down and shouted, "Lord Jesus, thank You! This is more groceries than I've seen in weeks. Hallelujah! Praise You, Jesus! Thank You for the groceries."

The neighbor stuck her head out and laughed, "Ha, ha, ha. I got you. I got you good! *God* didn't bring you those groceries. There is no God. *I* got you those groceries. Nobody is hearing you every day but me. I got you those groceries, not God." That grandma, undeterred, looked back to heaven and said, "Hallelujah, thank You, Jesus. Not only did You bring me groceries this morning, *but You made the Devil pay for them.* Thank You, Jesus! Glory to God!"

I want to make Satan pay. I want to make him pay. If you're with me, let's think about how we've been dealing with it prior to now. We moan, whine, complain, cry, and doubt. But God wants to flip the script. No matter how much the heat is on, no matter how much pressure comes, no matter what the temptation and the opposition, He wants to hear praise. We must decide today that no matter how we feel, we're going to praise Him anyhow. I'm going to sing about who He is and what He's done. I'm going to clap my hands. I'm going to lift my hands. I'm going to shout unto God! I'm going to blow my soul's trumpet! I'm not just going to do it inside the church, but out there when the battle is raging, when the attack comes, no matter what happens.

> *"We must decide today that no matter how we feel, we're going to praise God anyhow."*

I believe if God's people will start doing it God's way, if we will take Him at His word, then not only will we get the victory personally, I believe we can also begin to see the victory culturally. We can make hell back up. You may say, "These are the last days, and it's only going to get worse." Do you know what? They were saying the same thing right before the first great awakening, and they were saying the same thing right before the second great awakening. I'm ready for another great awakening!

Satan said about Job, "God, if you'll let me take his blessings, he won't praise you." Here in America, we are living in the most prosperous country on the face of this planet in all of history, and Satan says to God about us, "If you let me take it away, they won't praise you." I'm going to tell you something: I want him to find out quite otherwise. Take everything I have on earth and my name is still written in the Lamb's Book of Life. If you take everything I have, the Jesus Christ of Scripture lives inside of me by the person of His Holy Spirit. Take away everything I have, and the most important thing is what God's given me in the Gospel until Jesus comes, and that's still intact, no matter what. And some of us might preach in a prison one day, but God will even use us in that prison. Do you know how I know? Because He used a man named Paul all the way to the guillotine. And He's still changing lives today through the Word of God. We cannot lose! Especially when we do what God said and praise Him anyhow.

◆◆◆◆◆◆◆◆◆◆◆◆◆◆◆◆◆◆◆◆◆◆

PRAYING IT OUT

Father, I love You today. Thank You, Lord, that You still accept me as Your child when I miss what You've been trying to teach me. I have ignored the weapon of praise You've provided to me for far too long, and I have allowed the world to shape how I obey Your Word and how much I honor Your name. I repent of letting the fear of men and embarrassment keep me from boldly praising You aloud in every situation. You are good all the time, and I want to say so.

Thank You also for protecting me in this great war we are living in. Please keep things in perspective so I remain aware of the war that is raging, and make me willing to fight and knock Satan out of the air in the places where You have called me to live and serve. We're Your people and the sheep of Your pasture. Help us to know where the battle is, where it rages, and how to wage it in these days. We love You. We praise You in the name of Jesus. Amen!

When you wake up in the morning, a battle is raging. You recognize it, even if only subconsciously. Things are against you. Things go wrong. You can't stop being disappointed, worried, angry, or fearful, and you wonder why. We're living in a war. Ask yourself what some of the common battlegrounds are in your life, and try to consider how praise could help transform the typical outcome. Don't just think about it, either. Do it. Ask God how praise can help change your life, and do what God leads you to do. To cultivate a heart of praise, begin to thank God more often for who He is and what He has done in your own life, and look for promises in the Scriptures that you can rely on and speak back to Him in prayer.

CHAPTER 11
VICTORY IN THE STORM

*"There is no maverick molecule if God is sovereign.
If one single molecule is running loose, totally free
of God's sovereignty, then we have no guarantee
that a single promise of God will ever be fulfilled."*
– R.C. Sproul

*"Joy is the settled assurance that God is in control
of all the details of my life, the quiet confidence that
ultimately everything is going to be alright, and the
determined choice to praise God in all things."*
– Rick Warren

CHOOSING *JOY* OVER *HAPPINESS*

*Count it all joy, my brothers, when you meet trials of various
kinds, for you know that the testing of your faith produces steadfastness. And let steadfastness have its full effect, that you may
be perfect and complete, lacking in nothing.* (James 1:2-4, ESV)

As we dive into this chapter, we will find this content especially
applicable to all of us. Why? Because it's true what one has said:
Either you just got out of a storm, you're in one right now, or you
are about to enter a storm. Even if the content of this chapter
does not resonate with you personally right now, someone you
know who used to be in church and maybe claimed Jesus as their
Lord and lost their faith (or are on the verge of losing their faith)
needs this truth, because they are presently in a "life storm" of

some kind. So this fundamental tenet of victorious living is not *just* for your present reality or even what you may face in the near future. God wants to plant this word in you so you can take it to the other side of the exit sign in order to share it with someone who may go through a "life storm." God wants to use you in their life to minister life and grace to them in their time of need.

A brief aside vividly and humorously illustrates what I mean by "life storms." The story goes that a young boy walked up to the checkout line at a small, local convenience store. His only item was a box of laundry detergent, which he dramatically plopped onto the conveyor belt by the register. The grocery clerk eyed the boy curiously and inquired in a booming voice, "Your mother has you out shopping for her today, does she?" Respectfully, the lad replied, "No, no, I am buying this for myself so I can wash my cat tonight." The incredulous clerk patronized, "You don't need to wash your cat with laundry detergent. We sell pet shampoo on aisle three. Son, you might hurt that cat if you use such strong detergent for a bath." Invoking the wisdom of experience, the child defended his purchase, "I've done it before. I'll do it again. It's fine." With the transaction complete, the clerk and boy parted ways. Three days later, the same boy returned to the store to purchase a box, and the same grocer watched him suspiciously as the lad sauntered up to check out. With a raised eyebrow, the grocer asked, "No detergent today? Why the empty box?" In a somber tone, the boy explained, "The box is for my cat. He died, so I'm going to bury him in this box." Unable to restrain himself, the old clerk exclaimed, "Son, I said you should not have washed your cat in laundry detergent!" The boy sharply replied, "Mister, it wasn't the detergent that got him! It was the final spin cycle!"

We are grateful for the "cleansing wash" of Christ's atonement, aren't we? We need the toughest "detergent" for the toughest stains, and that is exactly what His blood removes: the stain of sin. But sometimes, I feel like the spin cycle is going to kill me. Do you ever feel the same? If anyone ever told you that by virtue of being saved, you are somehow going to be immune to problems, free from trials, or sheltered from every storm, they were painting an unrealistic picture (to put it mildly). Christ is our shelter *in* the storm, but the storm rages nonetheless. As a matter of fact, if you look around the world at other cultures, people's problems generally *begin or worsen* the day they give their hearts to Jesus. I am reminded of the lyrics popularized by Scott Krippayne:

All who sail the sea of faith
Find out before too long
How quickly blue skies can grow dark
And gentle winds grow strong

Suddenly fear is like white water
Pounding on the soul
Still we sail on knowing
That our Lord is in control

Sometimes He calms the storm
With a whispered peace be still
He can settle any sea
But it doesn't mean He will

Sometimes He holds us close
And lets the wind and waves go wild
Sometimes He calms the storm
And other times He calms His child

He has a reason for each trial
That we pass through in life
And though we're shaken
We cannot be pulled apart from Christ

No matter how the driving rain beats down
On those who hold to faith
A heart of trust will always
Be a quiet peaceful place

WHAT IS JOY?

The Bible has something to say about our trials and storms. I spend most of my time traveling for my ministry to participate in revivals, conferences, camps, Super Sundays, and various events, and I have observed a huge gap—a massive differential—between the message content and the manner in which event attendees actually live. It isn't an empty gap, either. It's often filled with problems, confusion, doubts, and struggles. Generally, these people hearing God's Word would love to be a witness for God, to be "fired up" again for Jesus, to live an overcoming Christian life; however, they have been overtaken by many doubts and fears. They wonder, "How am I supposed to run a race in a spiritual 'wheelchair?' I'm struggling just to keep my faith, much less share it." And this is a distorted reality for many people who sit in our churches week in and week out.

Perhaps you have heard the old adage, "When life hands you lemons, make lemonade." In the first chapter of James, God gives us a similar "lemons-to-lemonade" perspective. *"Count it all joy, my brothers, when you meet trials of various kinds..."* (James 1:2). Notice first that James addresses the readers as brothers, an inclusive term which implies they are fellow believers. These are born again, saved people. This is his family in Christ. He is in this fight with them, beside them, connected to them, and in relationship with them. These are people who have asked Jesus to be their Lord and Savior. If they died, they would go straight to heaven. To this "saved" audience, he says, "Count it all joy when you fall into various kinds of trials."

Please let me clarify: he did not say you must be *happy* about your problems. A distinction is in order because sometimes we think it is somehow more spiritual to be happy about our problems or that somehow we are blessed to be blissfully oblivious to our problems. He did *not* say we should be happy about our problems. I will be the first to confess that I am *not happy* about my problems. In fact, I have a favorite phrase found at least 120 times in the King James Version of the Bible: "It came to pass." Christian comedian Mark Lowry once quipped, "Either it will pass, or *you* will pass!" In regard to "life storms," I think we can all agree that we hope they come *to pass* and don't come *to stay*.

I would even go so far as to say that if you are happy about your problems, something is wrong with you! If you are happy about your problems, either the elevator doesn't go to the top, you're not rowing with both oars, you're not playing with a full deck, or the wheel is turning, but the hamster is dead. James did not say, "Be happy about it." He said to "count it all joy." **There's a difference between joy and happiness.** Happiness is a reaction regulated by circumstances. Joy is a chosen response regardless of circumstances. As a matter of fact, the word happiness comes from circumstances. It comes from the word "happenings." Have you noticed that when your happenings happen to be happening happily, you're happy? And if your happenings aren't happening so happily, you're not very happy at all, are you? When circumstances are good, your happiness meter goes up. In adverse circumstances, it goes down.

> *"Happiness is a reaction regulated by circumstances. Joy is a chosen response regardless of circumstances."*

James is saying something entirely different here. He's telling you that regardless of your happiness level and regardless of your circumstances, you can have joy in the face of it all. He says, "Count it all joy when you fall into various trials, knowing that the testing of your faith produces steadfastness (patience), and let steadfastness have its full effect, that you may be perfect and complete, lacking in nothing." His use of "perfect" here simply means "mature." So he is helping us understand that the testing of our faith helps us to become *mature* and complete in Jesus.

And I love the last two words, *lacking nothing*. This is where James drives the point home: the destination of joy's product of maturity is a place where we are lacking nothing!

ADJUSTING YOUR EXPECTATIONS

So how in the world do we "count it all joy?" How do you keep a lemonade perspective on the lemons in your life? How do you *live victoriously* through the storms of life? First of all, expectations must be adjusted. In verse two of the chapter, James writes, "... count it all joy *when* you face trials..." He doesn't say *if* but when. Please understand that storms *will* come, trials *will* arise, and sometimes it will seem as if life is slipping into reverse on this side of heaven. While this is generally obvious to most people, it cannot be overstated. I only emphasize this because it's not so obvious to many in the American Church. There is a myth, a lie, a false teaching and preaching that has permeated this westernized, air-conditioned, padded-pew Christianity to which we are accustomed. It presents itself as the notion that if you pray enough, if you are holy enough, if you are pure enough, if you give enough, if you sacrifice enough, if you believe enough, or if you are tired enough, then God is somehow going to make you immune to trials. **Nothing could be further from the truth.**

Maybe you have encountered another lie, and it goes something like this: You shouldn't even talk about your problems because it doesn't really help. We begin to engage in spiritual denial because we think God apparently wants us to be optimists, no matter what comes. Again, the survey says: FALSE. God does not expect endless optimism from us. And you know the difference, right? You've doubtless heard the definitions of optimists and pessimists, but let's review. The optimist says the glass is half full. The pessimist says the glass is half empty. The realist says,

"I'm going to have to wash that stupid glass." And that's what God is trying to do. God is trying to set us up to be realists. Let's just be honest. You know, you'll run into these people that say, "I have my quiet time in the morning because it makes my day go better." Listen, there have been times I've had my quiet time in the morning, and the whole day went to the Devil after that. Let's keep it real here. I don't have my quiet time in the morning because it makes *my day* go better. I have my quiet time in the morning because it makes *me* go better *regardless* of what happens in my day. There's a difference.

You might be saying, "But I thought God blesses us with better circumstances if we pray enough." Listen, if you want to know the truth, take a look at the history of the church, and you'll find out that sometimes—oftentimes even—it was those who were the most dedicated, most sacrificial, and most bold in their faith who were the candidates to get thrown to the lions. So God is saying to us, by saying "*When* you fall into...", be realists here. Adjust your expectations. *Trials* will come, no matter what. Peter said this about it: "Don't be surprised at this trial as if something strange was happening to you." Jesus said, "In this world, you will have trouble." And again, right here when we get to James, and he says, "...*when* the trials come, my brothers." So why is God doing that? Because God understands. God even understands human psychology. He made it. Getting us to adjust our expectations is the help we need most at a fundamental level.

> *"God does not expect optimism from us. God expects us to be realists."*

For instance, psychology describes an observable phenomenon that involves honestly adjusting our expectations in order to experience happiness. It's called the Stockdale Paradox, named after Admiral Jim Stockdale, who was the highest ranking officer in the Hanoi Hilton in Vietnam and who spent six years in a communist Vietnamese prison. He lived to tell about it. He was interviewed by Jim Collins, the man who wrote *Good to Great*, a classic book on how mediocre companies become standout companies over time. Jim Collins asked Stockdale the question, "How did you survive that prison experience?" The Admiral responded, "I refused to give in to the seduction of optimism." Jim was understandably confused, questioning, "How does that make sense? I would have thought that optimism helped save your life." Stockdale was adamant. "No, that's what killed all my comrades. They would sit in their cells trying to be optimistic, saying to themselves things like 'We'll be rescued by Christmas,' and Christmas after Christmas came and went without rescue. They all died of a broken heart. While I believed that we would be rescued one day, I refused to allow myself to hope or believe it would be anytime soon, and I embraced realism. **Realism saved my life.**" That's the Stockdale paradox.

This is how it works in your own life. Think about it; if you expect life to happen at a level nine or ten, but life happens at a level five, then you get depressed to level two because your expectations were dashed. But if you expect that life is going to happen at about a level five, and life happens at a level five, you get joy to level ten because you at least got what you expected. But if we are teaching that you're going to pray enough and serve enough and give enough that God is going to put this barrier around you, and you're not going to have any problems, then we are in trouble. If we thank God only for the sunny days and not for the storms, and if we just assume that it's all a big accident or God wasn't looking, then friend that sets Christians up to become the most easily disappointed people, causing us to lose our testimony at the time it should be the most powerful to a watching world.

Think about it. Say we have a lost guy who is far from God. He goes into a bar, and when he comes out, his car has been stolen. What does he do? Well, he drops a couple of cuss words, pulls out his insurance card, and starts the claims process to get a car to replace the one that was just stolen. Then a Christian goes into a bar...or maybe not? Let's go with something a little more Bible-friendly. A Christian goes into a Chick-Fil-A, and he comes out to find his car is stolen. What does he do? He hasn't even called the insurance company yet, and he's already asking big philosophical questions like, "Why am I being punished?" and "What sin did I do that has God so mad at me? Why did this happen to me?" His faith is literally in jeopardy because his car got stolen. Why? Because he's been *misinformed*—not by Scripture but by some popular TV preacher who wants to tell you that life is going to be a bed of roses because you're saved. I'm telling you, that's not the case. God, in His word, is trying to give you a biblical perspective, and the biblical perspective accepts that trials will come to your life. It even leads us to expect them. **You must adjust your expectations. It just might save your life.** Expectations must be adjusted if you're going to overcome storms.

SUBMITTING TO THE PROCESS BECAUSE THE PROCESS CARRIES PURPOSE

We have to understand the process. Go with me to James 1:2-3. He says, "Count it all joy when you fall into various trials, *knowing*..." which hearkens back to how we have been learning that **what you know determines how you go. Your beliefs determine your behavior.** So here is James saying, "knowing," which means, "I'm about to lay a truth on you. I'm going to give you something to know. I'm going to give you a piece of knowledge that you can carry with you into the next storm that will make all the difference." I don't know about you, but I want to know what that is. Knowing what, James? Watch what he says here —"...that the testing of your faith *produces*...." Let's just stop right there. The testing of your faith by the storm—by the trial— *is designed by God to be productive in your life*. Now this won't sound right to a lot of us. You might be thinking, "There's no way, man. If you saw my life right now, God is anywhere but in it. I'm telling you, it's like He's turned His back. Chaos reigns in my life. It's like everything is spinning out of control. There's so much destruction. There's not anything being built. I don't understand how you can say that the storm that's going on in my life is designed to produce anything good. It's destroying everything. How in the world could you say that?"

> *"The testing of your faith by the storm is designed by God to be productive in your life."*

The truth is, you don't see it, but it is. The storm *is* producing something in you. Listen, it's never uncontrolled chaos when God is in the picture. I don't care what it looks like. Let me help you understand. There was once a corn farmer in a county of corn farmers, and every farmer farmed corn. It was acres and acres of corn across this county. What these farmers would do is they would work their boys in the fields as you would expect, then in the heat of the day, they'd let their sons off. The boys would go down to the river together to hang out and play at the same spot each day. Then, when the sun started going down and it was a little cooler, they'd go back to the fields and work some more. Well, this one farmer had more corn than anybody—bigger fields than anybody and more money than anybody too—and he would not let his sons off of work in the middle of the day. Man, he just worked them and worked them to the bone.

Well, one day this rich farmer received a rebuke from one of his neighbors. The fellow said, "Man, you're working them boys way too hard. I mean, we're letting our boys go have a good time every now and then. Your boys would love to just get off work a few hours in the middle of the day; it's hot anyway. Let them go play down at the river with our boys. Listen, you're working them boys harder than we're working our boys, yet you've got more corn than anybody, and you don't even need all that corn you got." The farmer just looked back and said, "You don't understand. I ain't raising corn. I'm raising boys." Get this: it's not about the *corn*; it's about the *character*. It's not about what you see *around* them. It's about what's being produced *in* them.

Oh, it looks like chaos. It looks like God's not involved, but I'm telling you that everything that comes to your life has passed through the fingers of God. He allowed it, or He orchestrated it Himself, and without fail, without exception, 100% of the time, it is *always* designed by God to produce something of eternal value in your life. **If you're saved, you can't lose, no matter the size of the storm. It's productive. But you have to understand the process.**

Now what does he say? James says it's the *testing* of your faith. Now as soon as we hear the word "test," we think: classroom, white sheet of paper, filling out answers, and if you don't know the answer, you get an A, B, C, D, or F, right? That's not what he's thinking.

Funny story. One time a guy got pulled over by a cop because he was going a little too fast. When the cop went up to get his license and registration, he looked at the passenger side floorboard and saw three empty wine bottles. So what did the cop think? The driver had emptied the contents of the bottles, right? He was surely drinking and driving. But the guy is saying, "No, officer, I don't drink. I'm a juggler in the local circus that's in town for a few weeks. I juggle these bottles, is all. I don't even drink." Well, do you know what the cop said? "Prove it. Get out of the car, and bring the bottles with you." So the guy got out of the car with the bottles and started juggling. Then, an older couple driving down the road saw the man juggling. The husband in the car was watching the whole incident, and he said to his wife. "Gosh, I'm going to quit drinking, much less driving." His wife replied, "Why's that, Honey?" He just said, "Look at the tests they are giving now!"

It's not that kind of test! The word here, translated as "testing," has a similar word that, when used in the Old Testament, comes from the world of metallurgy, meaning those who fashion and work with metal, like a silversmith working with silver. What's that process? The ore is dug out of the ground unrefined, and they've got to use it and turn it into whatever implement. So let's say a silversmith is going to fashion that silver ore into refined metal that's going to be jewelry or silverware. What does he do? He has to *process* it. He has to get it to the point of being usable. He has to work towards purifying it. How does he do that? Well, he takes the unrefined silver and "tests" it, which literally means *to place it into a furnace*. And why does he place the unrefined silver ore into a furnace? Because he's mad at the silver? No. Because he wants to punish the silver? Of course not. It's about a necessary process.

He understands this: When you put unrefined metal into a furnace and turn up the heat, everything that is *not* silver begins to separate out. All the dross, all the crud, all the impurities begin to float to the surface. Once it's at the surface, the silversmith can easily remove it. When he scoops out the impurities, he turns down the furnace, and the rest of the silver exits the furnace ten times more beautiful, more usable, and purer than what went into the furnace. Are you tracking with me here? So when James speaks of the "testing" of your faith, he's talking about your faith getting refined so that it becomes—as Peter says—more precious than gold that perishes though tested by fire.

Listen, there are some things in our lives and minds that cannot be preached out of us, that cannot be counseled out of us, that cannot be sung out of us, or Bible-studied out of us, or fellow-shipped out of us; **there are some things in your life and in my life that can only be *burned* out of us by fire in the furnaces God orchestrates for us.** It is just as true a grace as His redemption or love. So James says, "Please understand that God has you in a furnace in these trials. There is testing of your faith going on, and it's *designed to be productive*. I know it hurts, but it's producing. I know it seems like loss, but it's actually gain. I know it seems like God left you alone, but He's deeply involved. God is up to something. It's a process. God wants to prove it and improve it so He can approve it."

◆◆◆◆◆◆◆◆◆◆◆◆◆◆◆◆◆◆◆◆◆◆◆

PRAYING IT OUT

Father, I don't often appreciate the testing of my faith. Though I hear Your Word say that I am meant to rejoice when trials come upon me, I rarely come even close. I am often obsessed with being happy instead of being holy. I care too much about comfort, but I recognize now that this is not what is best for my life. I recognize and repent of my belief that You are only good to me, God, when You make things easy. So I submit to Your process, to Your sovereign guidance of my circumstances. I love and trust You.

I want You to open my eyes and change my perspective on this. I invite Your testing in my life so that You can refine me and make me more like Your Son, Jesus. Please touch me with the flame gently but long enough to remove everything in my life that dishonors You, everything that keeps me from reflecting Your image. In Jesus' Name, I pray. Amen.

LIVING IT OUT

In our culture, it can be incredibly difficult to come to grips with the idea that happiness is not the goal of our daily life. But it isn't. God wants something better for us that doesn't depend on constantly shifting circumstances, and He calls it *joy*. Do you struggle to tell the difference between joy and happiness? Does your mind constantly evaluate your circumstances to determine whether you are going to be happy on a given day—whether it's going to be a "good" day? As 2 Corinthians 10:5 urges us, begin to take these thoughts captive this week and in the weeks ahead. When you find yourself saying things are just terrible or you're filled with anxiety about your circumstances not changing, preach the truth to yourself: Joy is a choice, you have a beautiful inheritance in Christ secured for you, and these trials can be used by God to produce eternal value in your life. Go to God in prayer with that heart, and He will change you.

CHAPTER 12

OVERCOMING LIFE'S STORMS: PERSEVERANCE IS A PRIZE

*"Mountaintops are for views and inspiration,
but fruit is grown in the valleys."*
– Billy Graham

*"There is no pit so deep, that God's
love is not deeper still."*
– Corrie Ten Boom

I was raised in church, and I believed the gospel at a young age—six years old for me. I genuinely understood the essence of the gospel. That's one of the great things about the gospel, that even a child can be saved. Isn't that just a great thing? When I came to Jesus at that young age, He *was* my Jesus, but He was *really* Mama's Jesus. You know what I mean? He was my God, but He was *really* the preacher's God. He was my Lord, but He was really Grandma's Lord. I mean, there is a degree to which—in the early years of your faith—you're riding the coattails of those who are more mature in Jesus, many of whom probably prayed and led you to Jesus. And that is okay because God understands that sooner or later, He's going to take you through trials, through storms, through valleys; He's going to take you to a hot place where He's going to bake ownership into your faith. He knows He's going to take you to a place where it feels like your prayers are bouncing off of the ceiling, all the friends that promised loyalty have left you, every prop you leaned on is getting knocked out from under you, and all the answers you thought you had aren't working.

It's in that dark place that God begins to reveal Himself in a way that He has not and could not any other way. All of a sudden—no matter how deep in the valley you've gone—I promise you, God will show up. And He'll do it in such a big way that when you emerge on the other side, He'll no longer be just Mama's Jesus; He'll be *your* Jesus. He won't just be the preacher's God; He'll be *your* God. You'll be able to say personally, "He's *my* shield. He's *my* buckler. He's *my* strong tower!" And you will *own* your faith on the other side of that valley in a way that you could not own it before. **Thank God for the valleys because they are productive in your life!** Understand, God has not left you alone. He's deeply involved and deeply connected to all the goings-on. He's producing something in your life.

TRIALS PRODUCE OWNERSHIP

My daughter and our only child, Gianna, is now a married adult mother, but when she was about five or six, my wife was homeschooling her as we traveled in ministry. We had sold the RV that we had lived in for eight years at that point, and I was trying to put down better roots for my family. My wife called one day saying something was going on with Gianna. I said, "Scarlet, what do you mean something's going on?"

She replied, worried, "It's like her short-term memory has just disappeared, and it's like anything we cover in school, she forgets the next day. Anything, I mean simple things, like two plus two, she's not keeping it. What's really bothering me are the blank stares."

I couldn't compute. "What do you mean?"

She continued, "Well, I'll snap my fingers because sometimes she's gone a minute, sometimes two minutes. It's like she's just not there. And the mood swings. We started seeing mood swings come that are *radical*, like a pendulum. Within 15 minutes, we go from panic to calm, from one end of the spectrum to the other. And not only that, but she has also started seeing and hearing things that are not there." This sounds like some scary stuff, right?

Well, one night, I remember going into our bedroom, and my daughter—who was seven years old at the time—was screaming her head off, back pressed up against the headboard of her bed, white-knuckled. She had the sheets around her chin and was screaming, "Daddy, Daddy, there are spiders all over my bed, spiders everywhere! Help me, Daddy!"

But I'm looking at her bed, and there's not a spider in sight. This kind of thing happened night after night after night. Then, insomnia started creeping in. She just couldn't go to sleep easily anymore. She couldn't get sleepy at 11, then it was 12, and then she was wide awake until 1 and 2 o'clock in the morning. Then it was 3 a.m. It wasn't just one night, but night after night and week after week.

At the time, we were working with "The Homeschool Doctor," a brilliant thought leader and researcher named Dr. Paul Cates. He would do cognitive testing on Gianna annually and prescribe our curriculum. He had been a researcher and lecturer for four decades and had seen everything under the sun. After running some assessments on Gianna, he came back to us and said, "There's something neurological going on; you need to see your neurologist. And for this kind of thing, there are only three I trust. I want to send you to the one in Chicago."

And I said, "Okay, we'll book that trip."

But Scarlet was anxious. She was saying, "Honey, I can't wait until your preaching schedule frees you up in a few weeks. We need to go now, even if I have to go by myself with Gianna, without you."

"God has not left you alone. He may be more involved than He's ever been, and He's producing something in your life."

So she got on a plane with our daughter and went to do the testing, and I got in my car to drive to Virginia to fulfill my next preaching agreement. I'll never forget March of 2008, walking out of that church in Virginia on a Tuesday evening after services. There was a voicemail on my phone. I saw my wife had called. I called her back. She told me we had a diagnosis. What was the diagnosis? "She has epilepsy." Epilepsy?

Now, I had had a very different picture in my mind of what epilepsy was supposed to look like. We'd never seen her eyes roll back in her head or seen her stiffen up and fall on the floor—nothing like that. As it turns out, there are over 40 different types of epilepsy.

My daughter had a form called temporal lobe epilepsy, which means that the "lightning storm" that is epilepsy is happening in the temporal lobe of her brain. The temporal lobe is the part of the brain that processes extreme emotions, from paranoia and panic to complete security and calm. She would swing between the two at radical frequencies. Not only that, it's also the part of the brain that decodes auditory and visual input. That's why she was hearing things that weren't there and seeing things that weren't there.

The temporal lobe also regulates the part of us that can calm down enough to go to sleep, which is why insomnia had set in, and now we were dealing with insomnia on top of trying to figure out which medication was going to work. Have you ever been there? The first medication for the first month made her so sick to her stomach that she couldn't eat. The second medication in the second month made her so lethargic she couldn't get off the couch. And her academic scores and learning capacities were going down the tube quickly. Finally, we got her on a medication that worked, but we were still dealing with insomnia. I remember looking at my daughter at 7-8 years old, knowing she needed at least nine or ten hours of sleep at night, and she couldn't go to sleep before one o'clock, but she couldn't sleep past 7:00 a.m. either.

I remember coming home from the road to see my wife, having tried to homeschool all day and having been up with her every single night. I'd take my shift and go in there, and I'd be looking at the little girl who's trying to figure all this stuff out, who has grown up on the road in ministry hearing all the sermons and seeing all the scriptures in homeschool every day. I remember one night, it was three o'clock in the morning, and I had my daughter in my arms down on the floor. My right sleeve was soaked with her tears as I listened to my seven-year-old crying out to God. She was saying, "God, if I ever get to sleep tonight, go ahead and let me die so I won't have to wake up tomorrow and live through this one more day." And there was preacher Daddy, and guess what? I had nothing. I had nothing for my daughter, who was inconsolable at a place her parent couldn't go. I had nothing for my wife, who was exhausted beyond belief and wondering why this had happened when she'd dedicated her daughter to the Lord and prayed for every possible circumstance. I had nothing to say. I'll be honest with you; I'm glad many nights I didn't say a thing because sometimes, when someone you love is having their soul dashed on the rocks of reality, the best thing you can do is keep your mouth shut and just be there. Pat answers, no matter how true, can feel like an aspirin being tossed at a victim of a car wreck.

But I'm telling you, **in that valley—in a way I wish I could articulate with words but can't—God began to show up in my daughter's life.** And He began to show up in my wife's life. And He began to speak to us in the secret places of our hearts. He began to buoy us up in exactly the places we thought we were drowning and sinking. He did perform some external circumstantial miracles, but He also offered us consolation and companionship in a way that no counselor could. I'm telling you, God moved in a way I cannot fully explain nor describe and in such a way that when we emerged on the other side of the storm, it had produced such an *ownership* of faith in my daughter's life—and our own lives for that matter. She doesn't believe because her dad's a preacher or because her mama homeschooled her in the Bible every day, but because God showed up in a dark valley.

In my own life, I began to see some things that were critical to help us become ready for the next, far bigger storm that I am not going to share about here. Let it suffice to say that I never thought something *that* difficult would touch us, and there's no way we would have made it through the big one if we hadn't made it through the other one I shared about. And what we learned could not be found in a book or classroom; it was from the presence of Jesus.

So just understand that there is serious ownership of the faith on the other side of that storm. I wish you could get it another way, but you can't. As an old poem goes:

I walked a mile with gladness

she chatted all the way

but I was none the wiser for all she had to say.

I walked a mile with sorrow

and not a word said she

but oh the things I learned that day

when sorrow walked with me.

"God offered us consolation and companionship in a way no counselor ever could have."

As a bonus to that story, in 2012, the neurologist said my daughter was healed of epilepsy altogether. She didn't need to take any more medicines. She took her last pill in December of that year. God does heal. Hallelujah! Glory be to God! He can do that.

A little Jewish boy once got mad at his rabbi because he thought the rabbi was misquoting the Bible. The rabbi kept saying, "God said, 'Place the law upon your heart. Place the word upon your heart.'"

And the Jewish boy said, "You can't be reading that right. That's not right. God wouldn't say that."

The rabbi didn't understand. "Son, what do you mean?"

The boy explained. "God wouldn't say to place it *upon* your heart. God would say to place it *in* your heart. Why are you telling us God said to place it *upon* your heart?"

And the wise rabbi replied, "Because placing it upon your heart is the best that we can do. But that's okay because if you place it upon your heart, when your heart breaks, the truth will fall in through the cracks." **Remember, we are talking about process. Expectations must be adjusted, yes. But *process* must also be understood and embraced.**

PERSEVERANCE MUST BE PRIZED

According to James, *perseverance must be prized*. Perseverance must be valued. You'll see why. Let's look at verse three of chapter 1 again, "knowing that the testing of your faith produces..." Produces *what*? *Patience*. Now that word "patience" is the same as the word "endurance." This is one spot where the King James gets it perfect. The KJV calls it "longsuffering." Really, the essence of that word is exactly that: *long* suffering—the ability to suffer long. It's a Greek term that is formed from two separate words: "remain" and "under"—meaning the ability to *remain under* something. It's the ability to remain under the weight, under the load, under the stress, without giving in, without giving up, without giving out. It's tenacity, longsuffering, endurance, or perseverance. Look at what he says about it. He says the testing of your faith produces the ability to endure, but you must *let endurance* have its perfect work so that you may be mature, *so that you may be complete, lacking nothing*. In other words, if we don't get the perseverance, we don't get the rest. Why? **Because the ability to endure is the connection point between what's going on around us and what God is trying to produce in us.** It's the ability to *stay under*. If you don't stay under, you'll lose it all.

> *"The ability to endure is the connection point between what's going on around us and what God is trying to produce in us."*

I've seen people like this, these "lacking nothing" people. Have you met one of them? Now, folks will say we never arrive on this side of heaven, and that's true, but some people get pretty close. I'm not saying I've met perfect people, but the kind of person I'm referring to, you'll know if you've met them. Have you ever seen somebody who's been walking with God for 40 years or more, and there's just something of the sweetness of heaven on them? They have such a wonderful disposition; they love everybody, and they just have that "peace that surpasses understanding" emanating from their person. It seems like when circumstances go south, it just doesn't affect them. Have you seen these people?

Upheavals in the world, economic crashes, terrorism, confusion and loss, and young people like me are running around, freaking out, "Oh no, what do I do?" And those folks are in the back doing what? Praising the Lord. Calm. Trusting. Loving. Worshiping. I'm like, "Don't you know there's a recession?"

They just say, "Sure! And I went through the *Great Depression!* I even lost just about everything, but guess what? God was faithful! I had kids, and I lost kids. God has remained faithful. My first husband was killed in the war, and God took care of us on the other side." And, honestly, they could go on and on. If we would just listen, we would see the power of longsuffering in lives such as these.

So I look at that, and I'm thinking, "I want to be like that *now*. How do I shortcut the process so I get there *now*?"

And God just says, "You *can't* do that. You cannot shortcut the process." So, how does God get us there at all? There's only one way: *Repeated exposure.*

THE NECESSARY PROCESS OF PERSEVERANCE: REPEATED EXPOSURE

Here's a funny story to illustrate. I'm not a hunter, but I was staff evangelist for a number of years at a church that was just full of hunters. Man, did they love to hunt. The head of this hunting crew was Barry Dugan, and he liked to try to get me in on it. I'd be out preaching a few weeks and come back to see Barry standing there at our home church on Sunday in camouflage, saying, "Come on, Scott. Are you going hunting with us in the morning? In the morning, we're all heading out for a hunt." He'd run into me out there in the vestibule of the church, with all his other buddies around looking at me, waiting for an answer to his urgings. "Come on, Scott, you're going hunting, right?" And the guys are just staring at me, dressed out in their own camos. It looked like the lobby of a Duck Dynasty convention.

This would happen time and again, and every time, I'd just answer, "No, Barry, I don't want to go hunting with you in the morning," but it didn't matter. Next time I was at church, he and his buddies would hit me up again like I'd never said a thing.

One time, I at least asked, "What time do you leave in the morning?"

He answered, "4:30 a.m." Now, I already didn't want to go hunting, but he really lost me for good at "4:30 am."

But this kept happening over and over again. If I came back again the next week or two weeks later, he'd come at me like he'd never heard me say no, as if we'd never had the conversation. "Hey, Scott, you know we're going hunting in the morning! You going hunting with us, Scott?! Come on, Brother, there's room in the truck for you. I have a gun you can use if you don't have one. We'll get you a fast-tracked license today. I know a guy. I'll have hot coffee ready in the morning. Are you coming?"

And I'm like, "No, no, Barry, I do not want to go hunting." This looked like it was going to be a perpetual problem no matter what I said back to him.

But then I got an idea after I'd had enough. One Sunday I went out through the vestibule at church, and all the hunter club was standing there behind their leader, and Barry lobbed his predictable invitation. That's when I said, "Barry, listen to me, read my lips. I'm *not going hunting*. Barry, do you know how excited you get at 4:30 a.m. on hunting days?"

He responded, "Oh yeah, for sure."

I continued, "You grab your camouflage, get your coffee, and warm the truck. You pull out; it's not even light yet."

His eyes lit up. He said, "Yeah, Brother, yeah!"

I said, "And it's 28 degrees outside, you drive out to 'no man's land' where you've got a deer stand thirty feet off the ground, and you're just waiting to nab you a big ten-pointer. You know how excited you get?"

Barry's got chill bumps at this point. A little drool was starting to leak out the corner of his mouth. He was like, "Yeah, My Man, yessir! I love it! I love it!"

I said, "Barry, listen to me! That's exactly how I feel about staying in bed!"

And that handled that.

I've got to tell you, I don't like 28 degrees outside. I don't like 30 feet off the ground. I don't like 4:30 in the morning. But Barry, he loves all of it. The very reasons he loves to go are the reasons I don't like to go! He loves 4:30 a.m. He loves 28 degrees. He loves driving out there in a truck in the dark, climbing up 30 feet off of the ground into a deer stand, and sitting for hours without comfort. He adores the whole experience. That does not deter him. Every aspect is a welcome part of the process. As a matter of fact, if you took all that away and just handed him a deer, he wouldn't want it. And if he went through all that and didn't kill one that day, he would just drive home in his truck grinning because he at least got to go deer hunting.

Now, how did he get to that point? Here's how: *repeated exposure*. He's gone at 4:30 in the morning a thousand times. He's handled 28 degrees outside so many times he doesn't even think about it anymore. He has climbed that high deer stand so much that it's like riding a bike. It's about repeated exposure.

WELCOMING TRIALS BECAUSE OF WHAT THEY ACCOMPLISH

So it is that through repeated exposure, God begins to do something in a person that only He can do, and *you begin to welcome the trial as part of the process towards the prize.* Listen to what Paul said in Romans 5:3-4: "We glory in tribulations." Think about who said that. Here's a fellow who was whipped, beaten, and stoned a few times – just for obeying God. I mean, here's the guy who was out obeying God to preach the Word, and God put them on a ship to go preach but told Paul before he even got on that he would shipwreck. He got shipwrecked as expected, barely made it to shore alive, and he was freezing. So he went to warm himself by the fire right after this horrific incident, and while he was trying to stoke the fire for a little more heat, a snake came out of the wood and bit him, hanging on his hand. I don't know about you, probably would have looked at the sky and shouted, "Ok, God, what gives?"

Instead, this guy says this: "We glory in tribulations." He was eventually beheaded, by the way.

> *"Through repeated exposure, God begins to do something that only He can do."*

Here's another statement. Listen to what Paul says in 2 Corinthians 4:17: "This light, momentary affliction is preparing for us..." You say, "Now Scott, there's Paul doing exactly what you said not to do. He's being an optimist. He's in spiritual denial. He's saying it isn't really happening, calling it light, momentary affliction when it's really heavy and weighty." No, he's telling the truth. He's being honest. When he says, "our light, momentary affliction," light and momentary are relative terms. They're true or false based on what you're comparing them to. Paul says our afflictions are light and they are momentary when compared to our "eternal weight of glory beyond all comparison."

What does that mean? Take the greatest sum of your pain measured across your whole lifespan. I'm talking about the deepest valleys, the darkest times, and the hardest and heaviest storms. Gather them all up, put them in one spot, and look at the sum of your pain. I'm telling you that **the sum of all your pain balled up into one lot of it is but a speck of sand compared to the mountain of joy and glory in the Lord in Heaven.** When we get there, we won't even think about what we had to go through in these valleys because of the glory that's going to be revealed in the presence of Jesus. It's all relative.

Later in the same letter in chapter 12, Paul begins to speak about the glimpses God has given him of the greatness of what is to come, literal heavenly revelations. He didn't even know if he was in the body or out of his body when they happened. But, reflecting further on that experience, he mentioned something peculiar that God did next. He said, *"lest I should be exalted above measure by the abundance of the revelations, a thorn in the flesh was given to me, a messenger of Satan to buffet me, lest I be exalted above measure"* (2 Corinthians 12:7). Basically, what Paul was saying is, "the vast awesomeness of what God has shown me is so incredible that if God had left me alone, I'd have been puffed up with involuntary pride." Now we know God values humility over pride, but Paul said it was so awesome he'd have been prideful. He couldn't help it. He'd have to have something outside himself applied to maintain humility about the experience. He continues on to say that God took care of it in this way: God sent a messenger of Satan to afflict him. (That'll mess with somebody's theology right there. Wow!) God *sent* trouble to Paul? Specifically, yet metaphorically, it was functionally some kind of "thorn."

Then Paul says that God gave him a thorn in his flesh to keep him humble. Again, to be clear, he's using metaphorical language. It wasn't that he got a splinter in his finger. It was a "thorn in his flesh," an affliction of some kind that bothered him at the core. Commentators debate about what the thorn was, with some saying it was his failing eyesight, others saying it was another physical infirmity, and still others saying this was purely an ongoing *spiritual* battle of some kind. But here's the important part. He said, "I asked God three times to take it away." I can tell you he asked many more than three times. Three is the number of completion. It's like Paul's saying, "The perfect number of times one can ask God to do something, the complete number of times, I asked Him!"

But all God said to him was, "My grace is sufficient for you." **Wherever you are in the series of storms in your life right now, God is saying that His grace is sufficient. His grace *will not run out* in the storm.**

Now Paul might have said, "But God, I feel *so weak* with this thorn." Here's the answer, the rest of the verse: "For My strength is made perfect in weakness." Now watch what Paul says, *"Therefore most gladly I will rather boast in my infirmities, that the power of Christ may rest upon me. Therefore, I take pleasure in infirmities, in reproaches, in needs, in persecutions, in distresses, for Christ's sake. For when I am weak, then I am strong"* (2 Corinthians 12:10). Paul had such a heavenly perspective on his storms that when they walked through the door, he could say, "Bring it on." Bring it on because it's achieving for me an eternal weight of glory, and it's making me more like Jesus.

WHEN HAVING A THORN IS BETTER THAN NOT HAVING IT

Now, we get confused about thorns. We will say, "Well, it's just my cross to bear." But if it's something you can't change, if you wish you could push a button and eject but you're stuck with that circumstance or that person, then I'm telling you that's not a "cross"—that's a thorn. A cross is voluntary, redemptive, vicarious, and that's a whole other sermon for another time. *But you don't choose a thorn.* Paul begged God to take it away, and He didn't.

So maybe you've begged God to take your thorn away, and He hasn't. What does that mean? Let me ask you a question: Is God good? *Yes.* Is God sovereign? *Yes.* Okay, read this carefully … twice. If God is good and God is sovereign, and He can't be anything else, and you ask God to take your thorn away, and if He doesn't take it away—in other words, if you ask Him to change the circumstance or the person and He doesn't—**the only thing that can mean is this: The presence of the thorn in your life is doing more than its removal would.**

The presence of the thorn in your life is producing more for His glory and your good than its removal would! Don't miss this! This is the perspective that will help you live better for Jesus with your thorns!

Here's the good news today. You can trust God. You *can* trust Him. You say, "It's dark." I know it's dark, but you can trust Him, and He is the light. You say, "It's been a *long* time." Maybe so, but you can trust Him; His love never fails. You say, "But it hurts real bad." Yes, I know, and He knows, and He has felt your infirmities. He's not a God who cannot identify with you in your struggle. The Word of God says, *"He was tempted in every way as we are, but without sin"* (Hebrews 4:15) and *"He learned obedience through what He suffered"* (Hebrews 5:8). He is Jesus—God in the flesh—who endured His own cross, but there's no crown without a cross. "Christ alone, cornerstone, weak made strong in the Savior's love...Through it all, He is Lord, Lord of all."

> *"The presence of the thorn in your life is producing more for His glory and your good than its removal would."*

What's your storm? What's your trial? Let's be honest. Our default reaction to these things is to whine, gripe, question, wonder, and doubt, but today, God says, "Believe." Today, God says, "Trust me. I have not left you alone. I have not abandoned you. It is not out of control. What is over your head is under my feet." That is God's word for you today. We have to stop letting our storms give us excuses to sin and to stop praying and to stop reading the Bible and to stop going to church and to stop sharing our faith. We just sort of let these things fall to the wayside of our lives at times, saying, "Well, look at what's happening to me right now." **We feel so justified sometimes in our complaints to God, but here's the truth: we are not our own; we are bought with a price.** Everything we are and have belongs to Jesus, and He knows what He's doing. He knows what He's doing! He's a carpenter, and He knows how to make use of the appropriate tools to take off our rough edges and to make us refined and beautiful and usable.

So maybe you need to look to your Father God today and

say, "Lord, I just want the right perspective. I want to persevere through my storm. I don't want to lose my faith in the storm. I want to gain *more* faith *in* the storm. I don't want my faith to be on the periphery of my life. I want to *own* it. I want it to be *in* me. I want it to intertwine with every part of *who I am*."

Don't let the Devil get glory. Let God get all the glory. Even the Devil can't do what he wants to do to you without permission from God. I'm telling you, God is in control, God loves you, and that cannot change. He is sovereign, and He is good.

Maybe you don't know this Jesus personally, but the ultimate question is this: Are you saved? Are you born again? Have you received Jesus in your life? No, that will not make you immune from sickness, disease, problems, and struggles; it won't. But I'm telling you, when you have Jesus, you have something in the storm that the world cannot claim, and it can produce something beautiful in your life. Choose Jesus and submit to His leadership in your storms so that you can be sure that you're safe, knowing that no matter what happens, no matter how big the storm—even if a storm takes your life—you'll spend eternity with God forever. Settle that today.

◆◆◆◆◆◆◆◆◆◆◆◆◆◆◆◆◆◆◆◆

PRAYING IT OUT

Father, I am sorry to say that I grumble and complain all the time about the storms that are touching my life. Lord, can I just say thank You for this thorn in my life? Thank You that it makes me look to You. Thank You that it forces me to come to You. Thank You that it makes me more dependent. Thank You that it makes me listen better. Lord, thank You for what You're doing. Use it in my life. God, I want You to engrave Your per-

spective on my mind. I want to get victory through this. I want to be mature. I want to be complete. I want to lack nothing. I want to be like Jesus.

Please come and work in me, adjusting my expectations so that I can see the world and my storms the way that You see them. Shape me so that I look like Jesus. Let Christ be formed in me through this process, and make my heart submit to the process. In Jesus' Name, I pray. Amen.

LIVING IT OUT

Maybe you are going through a rough time right now. If not, you will be before too long. Since God owns your life, and His love for you is sure, you can be sure that your trials are designed to produce something of lasting value in your life. Think back on your life and remember hard times that taught you to trust God. Jot down a list. Then take that list and thank God for the endurance and character that He has produced in you through those times. When your next trial comes, fight to go to God in thankfulness. There are also thorns in our lives, and if there is something in your life that you have asked and asked for God to remove, but it just won't go away, then ask God if 2 Corinthians 12:9 is His word to you. Fight to accept His answer.

CHAPTER 13

HOW OVERCOMERS STAY ON THE PATH: THE STANDARD IS SET

*"Keep this Book of the Law always on your lips;
meditate on it day and night, so that you may
be careful to do everything written in it. Then
you will be prosperous and successful."*
– Joshua 1:8

*"It is the knowledge of, and obedience to, the Word of
God that brings the best for every area of your life."*
– Paul Tsika, Scott's ministry mentor

God has given us a tremendous inheritance and armory to help us live the overcoming Christian life. We've covered much of it in this book. We know who we are. We know how to overcome trials. We know what weapons we have at our disposal. We know what to do with our money and with our lips. We can walk the narrow path with Jesus and live the overcoming Christian life. Now, we just need to make sure that we understand how to stay on the path for the long haul until, like Paul, we can say, *"I have fought the good fight, I have finished the race, I have kept the faith"* (2 Timothy 4:7). And we are going to begin in Psalm 119, the longest chapter in the Bible and right around the middle of all 66 books. But first, a pattern you're familiar with...

King David, a "man after God's own heart," right? We know all the amazing stories of his God-fueled victories, Psalm-writing, and bold faith. But later in his life, we read about his tragic affair with Bathsheba and the murder of Uriah. Wait. What?!

We might also know of perhaps a business leader known in their career for their integrity and faith, leading their company by Christian principles. Over time, other news starts developing. Then scandal. Corruption. Then an implosion of business and life.

Or think about that youth leader in a thriving church, passionate about mentoring young people. Over the years, he grows into larger ministries, more students impacted. He authors a few books, often speaks on conference stages. Some years later, he shocks everyone with a post on social media saying he's "deconstructing" his faith. He no longer even considers himself a Christian.

They are all like a ship setting sail towards a distant shore. At the start, its course is perfectly aligned with its destination. But if the captain of that ship makes even slight adjustments away from the course, trouble brews. Eventually, "Ship Wreck" or "Lost At Sea" is a headline in the town papers.

What happened? How does someone who is so clearly on the path get so far off the path? I will tell you this: **it does not happen overnight**. Just like spiritual growth is a process, getting off the path is a process. Often a slow one. It is baby step by baby step, the frog-in-the-kettle, something that oftentimes takes decades. Still, none of us are immune from straying off the path. So how do overcomers stay on the path? I take this directly from the text. Psalm 119, verse 9 says, "How can a young man cleanse his way?" That's the New King James. The NIV says, *"How can a young man stay on the path?"*

This is not just for young men, though. This is for anybody who is wanting to be an overcomer and stay on the path. We hear stories all the time about marriages that went off the path, ministries that went off the path, men and women who have gone off the path, and children who we've prayed won't leave the path but who still end up off the path. How does an overcomer *stay* on the path, especially in our context? How in the world do you maintain purity in an impure world? **Every single day, our**

godliness is under assault. It is our holiness as the chosen people of God that is under assault.

CHECK YOUR STANDARD

You can't even get your groceries out of the Wal-Mart checkout line without having to walk between two columns of carnality. We used to complain about the filth on the television shows. Now, the commercials are worse than the shows were. You take your family to the beach, and the closer you get to the coastline, the more lewd the billboards become. Don't even get me started on what gets posted to social. Our purity is under attack. So how do you maintain godliness in a world that hates godliness? How do you maintain holiness in a world that seeks to undermine holiness? How do you maintain righteousness in a world that mocks righteousness?

Well, I'm so glad you asked the question because the psalmist gives us an answer in verse 9. He asks the question, "How can a young man stay on the path?" He then answers, "By taking heed according to Your Word." **The Word of God must be our standard.** In other words, the standard for what is right or wrong in your life is not what is acceptable to society. The standard for what is right or wrong is not what the school system is teaching. The standard for what is right or wrong is not what your governmental party affiliation holds. The standard for what is right or wrong, good or bad, wise or foolish, is only one thing, and that is whatever God says is right, and whatever God says is wrong. His Word is the only standard that matters.

"The Word of God must be our standard."

Now, we say amen to that, but the question is: do we practice that? I believe we practice that far less than we think we do. And here's the reason: it's because we so easily substitute other standards without realizing it.

I remember when I got out of high school, I went on my first mission trip ever. I went with my church to Haiti. They told us, "Look, there's a lot of poverty in Haiti." I'd seen pictures of poverty, and I'd read about poverty, but I'd never *seen* poverty until I got to Haiti. People say, "Haiti's been bad since that earthquake." Let me tell you, Haiti was bad *before* the earthquake. Open sewers run through their streets. One can see tin roofs covering little shacks not much bigger than the kitchen pantry in your church building, and several might share one shack. One missionary told me some would have to take shifts sleeping so they'd have a place to live. That's poverty. That's where we were. You get the picture.

Well, we were at a missionary compound building doing stuff as you do on mission trips, and it was 98 degrees outside; it was unbelievably hot. One day, it broke 100 degrees. It was all we could do to stay motivated to finish our jobs around the compound for the two weeks we were going to be there. (Part of our project was helping finish a cinderblock wall around the mission compound.) Some of the leaders wanted to motivate our team, so they said, "Listen, if you get this much of the wall done by the end of the week, we're going to take you swimming." Now, that didn't really get my engine running that much because I hadn't seen any place in that country where I'd want to swim at all. I mean, they washed their clothes, bathed, and did other things all in the same river, so swimming didn't sound too good. But the leaders said, "No, no, it's a swimming pool we're taking you to; we mean it."

And sure enough, as it turns out, there was a French hotel on the side of a beautiful mountain just outside of Cap Haitien, where our missionary team had gotten permission to use the pool. We got really motivated when we heard that—the chance to swim in a *real* swimming pool—and so we met our goal. We finished out our section of the wall that week, and they said, "We're going swimming." All 35 of us jumped in the back of an Isuzu pickup truck, and they took us up the side of a gorgeous mountain, around a turn, and we saw it.

It was unbelievable. It looked like something out of a magazine. It was a sprawling resort with a big iron gate around it, and two guards opened the gate when they saw us arrive. We immediately began to survey. "Where is it? Where's the pool?" And there it was. It was a real, live, honest-to-God, in-ground swimming pool. The lawn was cut just right, lawn chairs were out, and palm trees were swaying in the breeze. We jumped off the back of that truck, threw down our towels, dropped our suntan lotion bottles, slung off our sunglasses, and stampeded toward that pool like a herd of water buffalo—all of us wondering who was going to be the first to jump in. I was fast, but I wasn't that fast. There was my friend, John, out front, the fastest among us. He got to the edge of the pool, was about to jump, and—ERRRRRRKK! He slammed on his brakes, sliding up to the edge of the pool, arms thrown out to the side, rotating rapidly in circles as he tried to throw his weight backwards to keep the momentum he'd gained from tossing him over the edge.

John just stood staring down into the pool. As the rest of us caught up to the edges, we all scattered around the pool looking in. And for a moment, we were glad we didn't jump in. Do you know why? No, it wasn't empty. There *was* water in the pool—if that's what you want to call it. It was a pool that had been fed by rain over time, not a spigot. Stuff was floating on the top, and stuff shifted around on the bottom. It was a nice shade of green. Dark green. Now, there was no such thing as chlorine, as a rule, in Haiti. Talk about disappointing!

We stood there on the side contemplating. My imagination started to embellish this whole scene. I was looking at the pool, thinking about the rats I'd seen in Haiti a few times since I'd arrived. They have rats in Haiti as big as your grandma's prize zucchini squash, that blue ribbon winner. I'm not kidding. You don't go deer hunting in Haiti; you go rat hunting in Haiti. They've got 10-point rats in Haiti. If you're driving and hit a rat in the road, it'll blow up your truck. So there I was, looking in that pool, and I could just imagine the scene: 100 or so rats with party hats on, holding cigars, eating shrimp and steak, just having a big old pool party, and I was going to swim in there?

I'll make a long story short. We *did* go swimming that day. But here's what had to happen. In order to go swimming, ease our conscience, and have a jolly good time, we had to temporarily suspend our "first world" standards for a swimming pool. **And we had to adapt to the standards of our environment, thereby easing our conscience and justifying our decision.** This is how that looked. See, by *Haitian* standards, that *was* a clean pool. By *Haitian* standards, that was the *best of the best*. They went swimming in the polluted river often enough. This place, the French hotel guarded by a big iron gate so only the elite could enter, was the best they had, and when you compared it to the environment, this was just so much better *by comparison*. After all, we were doing a lot better than anyone else who could be swimming just about anywhere else in the country.

Now, the same thing that our American missionary team did with that swimming pool in Haiti is the same thing that the average Christian in America is doing right now with the standards of the living God.

Instead of holding up the standard of the living God for our sexuality, for what comes out of our mouth, for how we raise our kids, for how we conduct relationships, and for how we steward our possessions, **we're adapting to the standards of our environment**—and that's not saying much.

I'm grieved about what our culture is applauding in this country because this country has been sliding ever since they said the God of the Bible is irrelevant and His Word is not for us. I'm telling you, we've been in a mess.

In the 1950s, America said, "I know what is right, and I know what is wrong."

In the 1960s, America said, "I know what is right, and I know what is wrong, but I don't care."

In the 1970s, America said, "I know what is right, and I know what is wrong, but nobody cares."

In the 1980s, America said, "I don't know what is right, and I don't know what is wrong."

In the 1990s, America said, "There is no right, and there is no wrong."

And since the turn of the last century, we've been making it up as we go—all while watching the degradation and decline. And all while calling it "progress." That is why every other god except the God of the Bible is the god in our culture, and as long as that is the case, we live in a nation that does not judge their sin by the lens of God's righteousness; they judge God's righteousness through the lens of their sin.

> *"We live in a nation that does not judge their sin by the lens of God's righteousness; they judge God's righteousness by the lens of their sin."*

In other words, to the eyes of the culture, if a person, business, or organization promotes marriage as God intended; it's a hate-mongerer against anyone who doesn't live that way. But that's like saying, "If you promote a healthy diet, you obviously hate obese people." C'mon. Let's see through that nonsensical perspective. What's at the core? Well, in the example of marriage and sex, basically, our nation says, "We want sex with no accountability, with no consequences, and we don't even want to be held accountable to raise the child that may come from the union that we had so that we can have more illicit sex. We want no one to interrupt that, not even with an opinion." That is why New York City and other places will stand and applaud late-term abortions, as happened recently at the time of this writing. In the 80s and 90s, even the most liberal politicians would say we wanted to make it "safe, legal, and rare." You don't even hear that terminology anymore. As a matter of fact, you wouldn't have believed it even a few years ago if somebody had told you that in our time, we wouldn't just be arguing late-term abortion, we would be arguing infanticide.

Do you know why? Because God's standard doesn't apply anymore. But let's be clear: it still applies to us.

The Bible says, "Where there is no vision, the people perish." Do you know what that verse really means? Motivational speakers always say that this means you need a good vision to pursue. That's not even what it means. The word "vision" there means "revelation" or "revealed truth." The word there, translated as "perish," means "to cast off restraint." So what that verse literally means is "where there is no revealed truth, the people cast off restraint." You know, the problem in the days of the judges in Israel was that every man did what was "right," but they did what was "right *in their own eyes*." So you had better be careful when somebody says, "I'm telling *my* truth. I'm into *my* truth." Listen, there's no such thing as your truth or my truth. There's just **the** truth. There's your opinion, but there's God's truth. They are not necessarily the same!

The fact of the matter is, there's only one way to live life successfully, and that is to do it according to the

manufacturer's instructions, and His instructions are found in the Word of God. It does not matter what the society that we're living in approves, the fact of the matter is, what was right when the Bible was written is still right today. What was wrong when the Bible was written is still wrong today. God has not changed His character; God has not changed His mind. And if we're saved and bought by Jesus, only God's definitions of right and wrong matter to us. This Word is our only standard.

> *"There's no such thing as your truth or my truth. There's your opinion, there's my opinion, and there's God's truth."*

The Word of God says in Colossians 3:16, "Let the Word of God dwell in you richly." Look, it's one thing to know it, but it's another thing to let it dwell within you. Do you know what the word "reprobate" means? "Probate" means "to hold out in front of," and "Re" indicates doing it again. So if something is reprobate, like when the Bible talks about sinners having a "reprobate mind," we get this idea of something being held out in front of something or someone else again and again. A lot of the American church today is reprobate in that sense. They come into a building every week, and someone holds truth out in front of them, then they go out and act like it never mattered. Then it happens all over again. Reprobate. It's being held out in front of us again and again, but we say, "I'm not going to do it; it does not matter."

I don't know about you, but I don't want to be a "reprobate" son in God's family. I want to be used by God. I want to walk closely with Him and to live by His revealed Truth. I don't want to be reprobate. I want to be convicted by the Word. I want to do what God says to do. Like James says, **I don't want to be just a hearer of the Word; I want to be a doer also.** So the only judge of my "right-ness"—the only judge of my righteousness—is not the public, and it's not a political party, and it's not even the Church. As a matter of fact, if somebody comes to me and says,

"Scott, there's an area of your life that I believe the Bible says is sinful," and calls me to repentance and accountability, then they are not judging my life by their own subjective lens. They are calling me back to the standard that's higher than both of us, that judges us both equally and objectively.

Hebrews 4:12 says that it's *the Word of God that judges the thoughts and intentions of the heart.* It's not my brother and not my church that judges those things inside of me. They may appeal to the Word of God, and it can judge us, but we must submit to the Word alone and live out what we know it says.

So it's not judgemental to say, "That's right, or that's wrong." It comes from the standard that was here before I got here and that is going to be here after I'm gone. It does not change, and I'm merely calling other brothers and sisters to account for the standards that hold us all accountable, which is the unchanging Word of God.

Look, Jesus said, "Two men built a house. One man built his house on the rock. The other man built his house on the sand. Waters began to rise around both houses. Storms rained on the roofs of both houses. Winds beat on the walls of both houses. And when the storm clouds cleared, only one house still stood—the one built on the rock."

AN UNSHAKEABLE FOUNDATION

Now, the disciples were smart enough that they went to Jesus after that story and basically said, "Jesus, that's a great story. What does it mean? I know you want us to be that guy building his house on the rock, so who is that guy?" Jesus said, "The one building his house on the rock is the one who hears these words of mine..." Well, we're doing good so far, aren't we? After all, you're reading this Christian book right now. We're in church on Sunday mornings, Bibles open, and *hearing* the Word. Jesus said that if you're going to build on the rock, you have to hear that Word. *But that's not all He said.*

Jesus said, "He who hears these words of Mine *and*—" You have to watch those conjunctions; they'll mess you up! "And" what? He said, "He who hears these words of mine and *puts them into practice.*" Well, there you go. We must submit to the Word alone and live out what we hear it say in order to build our houses on the rock. When we hear what He said in His love letter to us, and we do what He said in His love letter to us, we're building our marriages on the rock, our parenting on the rock, our finances on the rock, and our spiritual health on the rock!

How does this look functionally? One example might be Psalm 101:3, which says, *"I will set nothing wicked before my eyes. I hate the work of those who fall away; It shall not cling to me."* What does that mean? That means that the standard for what I watch and use for entertainment in my life is firm. If I'm a believer who loves Jesus, I want to be a light shining as a star in a black night. What that means is I'm not going to watch Game of Thrones because Game of Thrones is pornography, and God said in Psalm 101:3 that the standard is, "I will set nothing wicked before my eyes." So I'm not going to look at it.

Another example. The Bible says there's a standard for what comes out of your mouth too. Ephesians 4:29 says, *"Let no corrupt word proceed out of your mouth."* That sets the standard for what I talk about with the person cutting my hair when I'm sitting in the chair and they start to gossip. That sets the standard for what kind of joke I will or won't tell at work. That sets the standard for what will come out of my mouth when the hammer hits my thumb. That sets the standard so that my mouth is not meant to speak anything *"...but what is good for necessary edification, that it may impart grace to the hearers."* That's the standard.

Friend, let's face it: we have fallen far from God's holiness in the church. Vance Havner said, "The church has become so worldly, and the world has become so churchy, you can't even tell the two apart." But in my own walk, I can honestly say I have never regretted letting the Word of God set the standard for any area of my life, but I have borne much regret over violating that standard. Make the Word your standard, and you will never regret it.

> *"Life works best when you build it according to the manufacturer's instructions."*

Now, none of this means that it'll be *easy* to let the Word of God be your standard. It doesn't mean your flesh will like it. But hearkening back to the last few chapters, knowing our identity in Jesus, knowing that Jesus with all His light lives inside of us, you'd better believe He'll enable you, equip you, and move in you to obey His own Word. Listen, *we are not smarter than God.* I'm telling you, we are made by Him, and He gave us the instructions. Life works best when you build it according to the manufacturer's instructions. Let the Word of God "dwell in you richly." Let it be your exclusive, ultimate, final, and only standard of what's good, right, and best in and for your life.

THE SECRET OF THE WHOLE HEART

The Psalmist didn't stop there, though, in this Psalm 119 passage. Overcomers can stay on the path by making the Word of God their only standard, but they also make the God of the Word their heart's passion. Go to verse 10. "With my whole heart, I have sought You." Now, you know when he uses that word "heart," he doesn't mean that little red muscle that sits inside of our chest pumping blood through our body. When the Bible talks about "heart," it's talking about the seat of your mind, your will, and your emotions. When the Bible uses the word "heart," it's using that word to refer to one of those three things or all three at one time: your thinker, your chooser, and your feeler. So the author is saying, "With all of my mind, I'm seeking You. With all of my volition, I'm seeking You. With all of my emotions oriented towards You, I am seeking You. I refuse to be distracted by position. I refuse to be distracted by possessions. I refuse to be distracted by power." Don't forget, this is the king of a nation saying that. He had access to plenty to keep him distracted. He said, "All that other stuff doesn't matter. What matters is You, God."

By the way, any shiny thing you think is going to satisfy your life, anything you think you can buy with money, anything you think you can get in a relationship, and anything you think you can impress somebody and get—it won't satisfy. **Whatever you think is going to do it for you won't do it like Jesus.** The fact is, He is the satisfaction of your soul. The Westminster catechism had it right: "What is the chief end of man? What is your purpose in life? To glorify God and enjoy Him forever." That's why we live. That's why there's air in your lungs. That's why there are brainwaves in your head right now, to glorify God and enjoy Him forever. So we glorify Him by living out His standard, and we enjoy Him by making Him our passion.

> *"We glorify God by living out His standard, and we enjoy Him by making Him our passion."*

I remember when I was growing up that Saturday was house-cleaning day for my mom. There were dust pans flying, Pledge everywhere, vacuum cleaners going, and she'd be saying, "Come on, Scott, it's time to clean the house." But while cleaning the house was a priority for Mom, Bugs Bunny was the priority for me. Looney Tunes, here I come. Mom would be up Saturday at maybe 6:00 or 7:00 a.m., and she'd be in the kitchen working on stuff. So I'd sneak past the kitchen, go into the den, and turn the TV on to watch my Looney Tunes. I was zoned in. Sooner or later, every Saturday, she'd hear the TV on, realized I'd finally gotten out of bed, and she'd come into the room where the TV was on. She'd look at me and push her glasses up by the corners using the back of her yellow-gloved wrist. Then, out of her mouth would come the list. She would say out loud the list of chores and tasks that I was to carry out throughout the afternoon. Why? Because that was my job. How often did this happen? Every Saturday. But I'd miss every bit of it. I'd find myself in the kitchen 30 minutes later saying, "What did you tell me to do again?" Why didn't I remember? Because when she told me I was watching Bugs Bunny, and when I was watching Bugs Bunny, *nothing else existed*. There are only so many brain cells in this head, and they can only really concentrate on one thing at a time. My mom was telling me all that stuff, and I wasn't listening; I have what you call a *one-track mind*. Here's what David basically said in the Psalm if you paraphrase it, "I have a one-track mind. You could put neon signs around me, bells and whistles, and you could entice me with all you've got, but it isn't going to work. Why? Because with my whole heart, I seek God. With my whole heart, I'm after Him." With how much of His heart? The whole. That means *all* of it.

Are you a "whole-hearted" devotee? A whole-hearted seeker? A wholehearted pursuant of the Lord Himself?

◆◆◆◆◆◆◆◆◆◆◆◆◆◆◆◆◆◆◆◆◆◆

PRAYING IT OUT

Heavenly Father, I am glad You are still bearing with me while I have neglected Your Word in my life. I am often the one James described who was a hearer of the Word only, and not a doer. From now on, I want to be a doer. I want to see You make the Word my standard. Make me strong by Your Son living in me, and have me stand on Your Word in the face of temptation to

conform to the world. Do it in every area of my life, in my rela-
tionships, in my finances, at my job, and when I'm home enter-
taining myself. I ask You to give me a clean heart to seek You.
By Your Word of power that creates new things, create in me
a desire to commit to Your Word and seek You with my whole
heart. In Jesus' Name, I pray. Amen.

LIVING IT OUT

Be honest with yourself. Think about recent times you have read
the Word of God or heard a sermon sharing God's standards with
you, and you have essentially ignored what God said and continued to live the same way you did before. How often does this
happen? What are the habits, the rituals, the flesh defaults, the
tendencies, the patterns that stand in the way of faithful obedience
to God's standards? Have a candid conversation with the Lord
where you accept that He has promised, *"If we confess our sins,*
He is faithful and just to forgive us our sins and to cleanse us
from all unrighteousness" (1 John 1:9). Because of this promise,
come clean, and ask God to put in your heart a genuine desire to
"tremble at His Word," as Isaiah 66 says is His desire for us. Begin
to meditate on Psalm 119, and spend some time there, discussing
your level of obedience with God in specific areas of life like your
relationships, finances, and job, asking Him to "work in you to
will and to do according to His good pleasure."

CHAPTER 14

HOW OVERCOMERS STAY ON THE PATH: A SPOTLESS BRIDE

"Holiness is nothing less than conformity to the character of God."
— Jerry Bridges

"Give me one hundred men who fear nothing but sin, and desire nothing but God, and I care not a straw whether they be clergymen or laymen; such alone will shake the gates of hell and set up the kingdom of heaven on earth."
— John Wesley

"How little people know who think that holiness is dull. When one meets the real thing...it is irresistible."
— C.S. Lewis

When it comes to seeking God with our whole heart, the hardest part is making sure that we keep our heart from being devoted to other things. There's a verse in Scripture, Proverbs 4:23, that says, "Above all else, guard your heart, for everything you do flows from it." (NIV)

In other words, guard your heart because the person who influences your heart determines how you walk, how you talk, where you go, the friends you choose, the activities you engage in, and everything else in your life. So guard that heart of yours! To stress the matter, he says, "Above all else!"

Our culture doesn't understand that, do they? Our young girls and boys who are starting to date don't understand heart-guarding. We talk about a verse like Psalm 101:3 about protecting our eyes to protect our heart. Well, what if you wrote it out on a 3x5 card and taped that verse to your television? "I will set no unclean thing before my eyes." What if our girls and guys went on a date, and the first thing they did when they got in the car was tape a card up onto the dashboard with God's standard that says, "Flee sexual immorality." We set the standard. Now let's go, baby, it's time for pizza. Right? I told students at a camp once where I was preaching, "Next time you girls go on a date, just take that big family Bible, and put it right between you. Then he's at least got to go through Matthew, Mark, Luke, and John to get to you."

The point is this is a practical exercise. You take the standard, you apply it to your life situations, and you guard your heart. The world doesn't understand guarding your heart, but David said, "With my whole heart, I've sought You," so that means he guarded his heart. "Whole heart" seeking means he's not leaving part of his heart vulnerable to seeking what it shouldn't.

WHAT GUARDING YOUR HEART LOOKS LIKE

I remember when I was in seminary, we lived in a little three bedroom apartment. There were four other roommates and myself, and even though it was only maybe 900 square feet in total, it had three levels. There was a bottom level with two bedrooms, a middle level with a den and kitchen, and a top level with the third bedroom up some narrow stairs by itself, like a loft.

One night, I was the last one to get in bed, and every guy was out for the count; they were sleeping, two guys to a room, and my roommate was already on the bottom bunk, out cold. I finished studying, turned out the light, climbed up onto my bunk, and was about to go to sleep when I heard, all of a sudden, the pitter-patter of raindrops on the window. I remembered that I had left my windows down in my car, and now it was raining. So I got back up, threw on some warmer clothes, went up the short half-set of stairs to exit through our main door, and walked outside to roll up the windows of my car.

Now, I was only gone for maybe a minute and a half. I went out quietly with every guy asleep in bed.

When I came back in, mass chaos had broken out in our apartment. Every guy was out of bed, running around in the dark, wielding baseball bats and golf clubs, and they were yelling, "Somebody's in the house! Somebody's in the house!"

I was thinking, "What in the world has happened in this place?" Then I started putting two-and-two together. I realized that they had been out cold, probably dreaming, all snug in their beds, visions of sugar plums dancing in their... Anyway... So all they knew was that they had heard a door shut when I went out, and their little bitty eyes popped open, and for some stupid reason, the first thought in their minds was, "Somebody just broke in!" So they jumped out of their beds, grabbed the nearest weapons they could find—baseball bats and nine-irons—and were about to kill each other, running around, bumping into each other in the dark, guarding stuff that, quite frankly, was of little value. (We were poor seminary students, after all.)

Now that I had figured all this out, I was down in the foyer just laughing... but laughing pretty hard. Finally, one of them caught me and said, "Hey, man, what are you doing?"

I said, "I'm laughing at you."

They said, "Are you crazy? What's wrong with you? Where's your weapon?"

I said, "I don't need a weapon except to protect myself from you!"

I said, "Guys. Listen, y'all are all confused right now, but here's the deal—I was the last one in bed; I heard it starting to rain, and so I just went outside to roll up the windows in my car."

They said, "You just went outside?"

I said, "Yes."

"Just now?"

"Yes."

They said, "Well, when you went out, did you see somebody come in?"

Good grief.

Have you ever seen something dawn on four people at the same time? It's like a big wet blanket just sort of came in and fell on them.

They started laying down their weapons; it got quiet; then one of them broke the silence and said, "We're so stupid."

Then another one began to get embarrassed. He said, "Uh, fellas. We aren't going to tell anybody about this, are we?" So jocularity gave way to embarrassment, and embarrassment gave way to pride.

One said, "Wait a minute, fellas. I've been thinking. We've learned a valuable lesson tonight. There's nothing here to joke about, nor should we be embarrassed. We can sleep soundly in our beds every night because we have learned that *nobody* will ever successfully break into our apartment, or they will face death by nine-iron."

It looked like foolishness at the time, but we could've held our own had there been an invasion. Why? We were *guarding* our apartment *"with all diligence"* and *"above all else."* You see, the Bible says to guard your heart with that kind of diligence. If you guard your heart with that kind of diligence, then you need to be prepared to be called foolish. Think about it. You're saying, "Wait a minute; I'm not going to watch just any ol' kind of movie because my eyes belong to Jesus. I'm not going to just tell any ol' kind of joke because my mouth belongs to Jesus. I'm not going to just go to any ol' establishment because my feet belong to Jesus. I'm bought with a price, and I live by His standards. It isn't my rulebook. It's His rulebook. It isn't the school's rulebook. It's His rulebook. It isn't my peers' rulebook; it's His rulebook. He sets the standard," and you're holding that mindset in the midst of a culture that "does what's right in its own eyes. It's totally worth it. But be prepared to be misunderstood at best or maligned at worst.

Many of those with whom you work, go to school, or even live will not see it the way you see it when you see life through a spiritual, biblically based lens. Be prepared for your righteousness to be judged by the lens of their fallenness. Jesus set our expectations for living in this world when He said, "If they persecuted Me, they will persecute you."

David said, "With my whole heart I've sought You," not with 75 percent of it, and not with 90 percent of it, but with all of it. My whole heart.

"Yeah, I get it. I see God with my heart."

I hope so. But let's stop a moment.

Is your Bible dusty while your TV is warm? That's a red flag.

Do you have time to binge-watch Netflix but no time for prayer? That's a red flag.

Do you scroll, scroll, scroll, scroll, scroll, scroll, scroll, scroll on your phone but don't read, read, read, read, read the Word? Yep. Red flag.

FINDING (AND HOLDING ONTO) GOD

Since David said he sought God with his *whole* heart, I believe he found God. Why do I believe that? Because God made a promise in Jeremiah chapter 12. Here's what He said: "You will find Me if you search for Me with all your heart." I don't know about you, but I'd say that's good news right there.

> *"God made a promise: He will be found if you search for Him with all your heart."*

David said, "With my whole heart, I've sought You." God says, "Well, you'll find Me then, sure will—if you search for Me with all Your heart." James said, "Draw near to God, and He will draw near to you!" That's a promise for you from the Word of God.

DESPERATION DELIVERS RECIPROCATION

I remember when the first grandchild was born into the family, my nephew Blaine. I remember when Blaine was at that age where he could walk but couldn't talk yet. Do you know that age? They usually walk around the house with no shirt, no shoes, and just a diaper that's half hanging off that probably has something in it. Here's the thing about kids that age: they can't talk yet, but they can understand what *you* say. Or at least some of it. The way I knew he understood some of what I was saying was how he would act every time I would say, "I'm gonna get ya; I'm gonna get ya!" And He'd speed off in the opposite direction of me. He couldn't say that, but he knew what that meant when I said it.

And usually, when he was running away from Uncle Scott, he was running *toward* Papaw. Usually, this would happen at my parents' house; they'd be keeping him for a while, and I'd be

212

coming through, and I'd go spend some time with Blaine. I'd chase Blaine around the house, and he'd always head for Papaw, eyes big, mouth open, and arms straight ahead, desperately reaching for Papaw. Why? Because he understood that no matter how full Papaw's hands were and no matter how distracted Papaw might seem, when Papaw saw Blaine running toward him with desperate arms outstretched, Papaw's hands would get empty and open quick. Papaw would make a beeline for that boy. "Come on, Blaine! Come on, Blaine, I'll protect you from Boogeyman Scott. Come on!"

It really was a sweet thing to watch. But I'm going to remind you here—God is 10,000 times better than any granddaddy or daddy on the planet. God is 10,000 times better, and when you seek Him with all your heart, when you turn your eyes toward Him and throw your arms forward in dedicated reach, it may seem like He hasn't been paying attention, but when God sees your desperation, I'm telling you, He opens His arms, scoops you up close, and there's restoration! God made a promise: *He will be found if you search for Him with all your heart.*

PRONE TO WANDER

I believe David had a hold of God. I believe that not just because of God's own promise but because he wrote the next line in verse 10. He says, "Oh, let me not *wander*. Oh, let me not *stray* from Your commandments—from Your standard. Let me not *drift*." Now, why would he say that? Here's why: *because it is our tendency to wander.* It is our tendency to stray! Is it not? The gravitational pull is not toward God this side of Heaven; it's usually away from Him. We're like a boat by the dock. There had better be a rope attached because it tends to drift out, not in.

So David prays, "Lord, let me not wander." We might say:

"The culture is pulling on me; don't let me stray. Hollywood is pulling on me; don't let me stray. My friends want me to lower my standards..."

You know, so many ministries are out there today trying to be palatable to a culture that has drifted away, and so they're pandering, forsaking the Word of God and trying to lower the standard. We need to remember God doesn't lower; He *lifts*.

Now, here's the big question: how does God answer that prayer, "Let me not wander?" It's simple. Here's how He does it.—Maybe you'll be in a Sunday service. Maybe you'll see a Scripture verse meme on Instagram. Maybe you'll just happen across a preacher on the radio when you're turning the dial and stop for a minute. Maybe you'll be in a worship service during praise and worship time, and the song lyrics are pouring off the screen. Whatever the instance, somehow, God puts His standard back in front of you right where you are. How many times does that standard He puts in front of you have something to do with where you are right now in a situation or circumstance? Anyway ... God brings something up, something in your life that violates the standard. This has happened to me so many times. He brings it up, and honestly, we feel bad most times about whatever it is. We feel bad about our sin, about violating the standard, and about all these mental gymnastics we've been doing trying to justify something being in our life that shouldn't be there to begin with, and God'll just bring it up. Here's what that's called: *conviction*.

> ## "We can get back to the standard just by heeding the conviction of the Spirit."

Now, watch this. What I'm about to describe is very important to note and understand. As soon as God convicts, Satan comes in right behind Him and puts a different spin on the situation. And here's what Satan says: "Aha, see? God is mad at you! You feel bad, and do you know why? God is beating you over the head because you blew it again!" I'm gonna tell you something—that is a lie from the Devil. I know it's a lie because **conviction is not an angry God beating you up because you blew it. Conviction is a loving God drawing a drifting heart back to Himself.**

The reason God brings up how you violated the standard is not to make you feel rotten but so you'll deal with the thing that has broken your fellowship with Him because God wants the fellowship restored more than you do. So He brings it up so we can confess and repent. And that's when we're reminded that He's the God of the second chance and the third chance and the tenth chance and the 20th chance. We can get back to the standard just by heeding the conviction of the Spirit.

I believe there's a whole lot of conviction going on in our generation, or there should be. If we in the American church have not totally numbed our consciences, this is likely happening because the Bible says in Revelation 12 that He's coming back for a spotless bride.

CAN YOU LOOK HIM IN THE EYE?

Jesus didn't say, "I'm coming back for an adulterous bride." He didn't say, "I'm coming back for a worldly bride." He said, "I'm coming back for a *spotless* bride." There's a good-sized gap between where we are now and that description of "spotless" as it pertains to being unsullied by the world. So what's in the middle of that gap? *Conviction.* Drawing us. Returning us to the standard.

I'm a traveling preacher and communicator, not a pastor, but I have done my share of weddings, and I love doing weddings because you have the bird's-eye view of everything. There's the groom and all his groomsmen in their rented tuxedos, and there are all the bridesmaids in those dresses that they paid for that they don't like and they'll never be able to sell on eBay. And they're up there waiting; everybody's waiting on the same thing. What are they waiting on? (Cue the music.) "Here comes the bride ..."

Now, you look at the bride, and you're thinking, "She doesn't look a thing like she did yesterday." Yesterday, she was stressed out, yelling at her mom, and had that old sweatshirt on. Today she's got the standout white dress, with every hair sprayed in place and pristine makeup. I'll tell you, I have *never* seen an ugly bride. Here's the thing I've noticed, though, about the bride when she's coming down the aisle. For the ones that I knew had maintained a pure relationship and saved themselves for their wedding day (even if they had made regrettable mistakes in their past before they met their mate), I could tell a difference. Those who put a premium on maintaining purity had this in common: when the bride came down the aisle, she could look her groom in the eye. She had a clear conscience. The Bible says we are the bride of Christ. And the groom, Jesus, is coming back for His bride.

You're a part of Jesus' bride, so here's my question for you: if He came back today, could you look Him in the eye? What does that mean? It means you could tell Him, "Your Word was my standard. Not my feelings. Not the cultural barometer. Not my political party. Your Word. And You were my passion, my heart-beat, my soul's desire. At times, I drifted, and at times, I strayed, but You were my greatest prize." Could you look Him in the eye?

You may say, "Scott, wait a minute. Nobody's perfect." You're right. But if you love Jesus, there is no room for *intentionally* imperfect.

"Well, Scott, everyone has some area of compromise. It's okay. It's just how people are. It's just how I am. It's just a thing, but it's no big deal. Besides, God overlooks it. He forgives me regardless."

Okay. I know many hold that perspective. And they limit the standard they seek to live out in their lives. But is that really fair to God, considering Who He is and what He's done?

Here's an example. Let's say you come to my house and surprise me with a visit. I say, "Come on in," and you sit down to talk to my family. So I ask, "Are you hungry; do you want anything to eat?"

You reply, "Yeah, you know what, I've been on the road a while, and I think some food would be good."

So I say, "Let's see what I have." I go into the kitchen, check out the fridge, and there is almost no food. The only thing I see in there is cheese and a dozen eggs. So I come back and say, "All I have are eggs and cheese. Can I make you an omelet?" You think that sounds good, so I go into the kitchen, get the dozen eggs out, get the big mixing bowl, and I start cracking eggs and dropping their contents into a bowl. One. Two. Three. Four, five, six. Seven. Eight. Nine. And on the tenth one, crack! Vapor! Smell! Stink fills the kitchen!

It's rotten.

It's already in the bowl.

"Well," I say to myself, "there are *nine good* eggs in there. I'll just leave it like it is. They'll never know!"

Now, if I served you that omelet, and you found out later that I served you an omelet with a rotten egg in it, would you consider me a very good host? Nope. Would you ever eat one of my omelets again? No way.

Let me ask you: What if *God* was your *guest*—and your *life* was an *omelet*? What kind of omelet have you been serving God? What kind of an omelet does He deserve? Have you been justifying the bad eggs and still serving it all up to Him?

Look, our standard is to be no less than the Word of God. Our passion is to be no less than the God of the Word.

But have you blown it? Good news—the great thing that sets God apart from every chef on the planet is that He can do what none of them can do. He can take your "omelet" just like it is, bad eggs and all, and make it pure and new again. You can bring it to Him just like it is and say, "God, I don't want it like it is. This is how I've been serving it to You, but I don't want it like this anymore," and He can make it brand new. You can be an overcomer who stays on the path. You don't have to become another statistic. You don't have to become another drifter. You can be who God says you can be, but you're not going to do it without these two things: making the Word of God your standard and the God of the Word your focus.

Jay Leno said this, "I'll do anything for the perfect body except diet and exercise." Too many say similarly, "I'll do anything to be an overcomer except the Word of God and the God of the Word." They just won't do it. You won't overcome without those two things, the Word of God and the God of the Word—your standard and your passion. Does God love you today? Yes. Will God forgive today? Yes. Will God let us start over today? Yes.

Just take an attitude of prayer and say, "Lord, where in my life have I stepped away from Your standard and justified something that is not Your standard that You want to address today?" I believe we can talk to God because I believe God speaks. Just offer that. "Lord, is there something I'm doing, something I'm thinking, something I'm looking at, something I'm taking, something I'm engaged in, or something I'm approving of that's against the Word of God? What did You want me to get from this chapter I've read today?"

Listen, you're asking that of the God who loves you and is ready with full forgiveness and grace to restore you. Let's be honest, most of us have something in our life that we know is against God's standard. So maybe today you go before God and say, "Lord, I'm going to lay that at Your feet. Today's a start-over day for me." If you think God isn't going to forgive you, just look at what He did with Peter who denied Him—cursing as he did it—three times! Look how fast Jesus restored him when He found him fishing after the resurrection. And that same Jesus will just as enthusiastically restore you.

Maybe your concern is this: "Lord, I get excited about so many things more than I get excited about You, and, Lord, I want You to reignite the passion of my heart." Do you think He'll answer that prayer? Yes, He surely will. Like little Blaine running to Papaw, can you turn your eyes upon Jesus, and stretch out your arms and hands to Him in desperation, and run back to God the Father today? He's ready. He's willing. He's waiting.

◆◆◆◆◆◆◆◆◆◆◆◆◆◆◆◆◆◆◆◆◆◆

PRAYING IT OUT

Heavenly Father, I thank You for Your clear Word. I am sorry that I just don't want to obey it many times. And it's not that You're not good enough or loving enough, it's just that I'm so easily distracted in this world with all the shiny objects grasping at my affections every day. Today, Lord, You are the One that is the most beautiful to me. You are altogether lovely. You are the greatest treasure of my heart. I want to return to You today. I want real renewal and revival in my heart to happen today. Lord, my arms are out, and my heart is toward You—maybe it wasn't yesterday, but now it is.

I don't want to go down the cesspool stream with the culture. I want to be shining like a star on a black night, and I want You to get glory from my life. I want to enjoy You forever, and I don't want to be someone who lowers Your standards; I want to be someone who lifts up. Your Word says, "If we confess our sins, Jesus is faithful and just to forgive us our sins and cleanse us of all unrighteousness." I lay hold of that promise today and trust You to fulfill it, Lord. By Your grace, make me an overcomer who stays on the path for the long haul until I meet You at that wedding feast as part of Your spotless bride. In Jesus' Name, I pray. Amen.

LIVING IT OUT

How did you answer the question earlier in the chapter about our coming wedding day with the Lord Jesus? Could you look Him in the eye when you walk down the aisle to meet Him at the wedding supper of the Lamb? If, like many of us, you are "prone to wander, Lord, I feel it, prone to leave this God I love," then remind yourself daily of God's sure love for you as proven by the cross, and grab some key Scripture sections to keep it on your mind in the days ahead. Commit to Him today, asking God to create a deep devotion in you that is worthy of Him. Be honest with yourself about what you have been serving God. Have you been offering Him yourself but without aligning your life with His standard? As you set out to live the overcoming Christian life, the most important thing you can do is reconcile with your Father and start clean, letting Jesus remove every blemish on your character. Only He can keep you on the path.

APPENDIX

UNDERSTANDING SALVATION: WHY IT'S IMPORTANT AND HOW TO GET IT

Your salvation starts with God's purposes. God's glory is the ultimate reason behind everything in existence. The Bible teaches that the chief purpose of mankind, including you, is to glorify God and enjoy a fulfilling relationship with Him forever. However, because of sin, this purpose has been disrupted, and humans are separated from experiencing God's full glory.

Salvation through Jesus Christ is essential because it restores us to our true purpose. By accepting Jesus as our Savior, we are forgiven and brought back into a right relationship with God. This allows us to live lives that glorify Him, reflecting His love and grace to others, living in our unique purpose, and enjoying His presence now and for eternity. Salvation is not just about securing a place in heaven; it's about living a life that displays God's glory in every way.

In light of this, it's important to understand why we need to be saved and how we can accept this wonderful gift.

WHY WE NEED SALVATION

1. **Sin Keeps Us Away from God**: The Bible says that everyone has sinned and that keeps us away from God (Romans

3:23). Sin makes a barrier between us and God, and it means we could be away from Him forever.

2. **God's Rules Say Sin Must Be Punished**: God is just and fair, so sin must be punished. The Bible tells us that the punishment for sin is death, and not just dying, but being away from God forever (Romans 6:23).

3. **God Loves Us and Made a Way Out**: Even though there must be a punishment for sin, God loves us so much that He made a way to save us. John 3:16 says that God sent His only Son, Jesus, so that anyone who believes in Him won't be punished but will have eternal life. Jesus paid for our sins when He died on the cross, and that fixes the gap between us and God.

HOW TO BE SAVED

1. **Admit You Need Jesus**: The first step is to admit you're a sinner and you need God's forgiveness. You can't save yourself by just being good.

   - Romans 3:23 - *"For all have sinned and fall short of the glory of God."*
   - Ephesians 2:8-9 - *"For by grace you have been saved through faith. And this is not your own doing; it is the gift of God, not a result of works, so that no one may boast."*

2. **Believe *on* Jesus**: You need to believe that Jesus is your Savior, that He died for your sins, and He came back to life. This shows He beat death and can give you eternal life with God.

   - John 3:16 - *"For God so loved the world, that he gave his only Son, that whoever believes in him should not perish but have eternal life."*
   - Romans 10:9 - *"If you declare with your mouth, 'Jesus is*

Lord,' and believe in your heart that God raised him from the dead, you will be saved."

3. **Express Your Regret Over Your Sin and Turn from It**: Saying you're sorry means you agree with God that you need to change and stop doing wrong things. You also need to believe in your heart and say with your mouth that Jesus is your Lord.

   - Acts 3:19 - *"Repent, then, and turn to God, so that your sins may be wiped out, that times of refreshing may come from the Lord."*
   - 1 John 1:9 - *"If we confess our sins, he is faithful and just and will forgive us our sins and purify us from all unrighteousness."*

4. **Surrender Your Life To Jesus**: Salvation is a free gift from God, and you get it by trusting in Him. Ask Jesus to come into your life to be your Lord and Savior, and accept His forgiveness and love. Do this with a mindset of complete surrender to His will for your life.

   - Romans 6:23 - *"For the wages of sin is death, but the gift of God is eternal life in Christ Jesus our Lord."*
   - John 1:12 - *"Yet to all who did receive him, to those who believed in his name, he gave the right to become children of God."*

If you're looking into what it means to be a Christian or if you want to understand better how to be saved, I suggest watching a simple video I created that talks more about these ideas. It's clear and easy to understand, and it helps you learn how to start this amazing journey with God.

Navigate to https://www.snsministries.org/goodnews or scan the code below.

If you're ready to receive Christ in your life right now, then perhaps the following prayer expresses the desire of your heart.

"Dear God, I know I'm a sinner, and I ask for your forgiveness. I believe Jesus Christ is Your Son. I believe that He died for my sin and that you raised Him to life. Right now in the best way I know how to ask, please come into my heart and be my Savior and King of my life. I trust Jesus to save me from my sins and give me a place in eternity with Him. I surrender my life to follow Him as Lord, from this day forward. Fill me with your Holy Spirit, guide me and help me to do your will. I pray this in the name of Jesus. Amen."

If you prayed this prayer, please let me know by dropping me an email to scott@snsministries.org. I would not only love to know about it, I'd like to send you some materials that will help you grow. God bless you.

are we in your feed?

▶ @SCOTTNEWTONLIFE

📷 @SCOTTNEWTONLIFE

f /SCOTTNEWTONLIFE

"My calling is to deliver biblical insights that help you mine the best out of what God put in your life in the face of the modern world."

Scott

ABOUT THE AUTHOR

Other than being a husband, father and now a grandfather, Scott Newton Smith is a dedicated revivalist and educator in the principles of victorious Christian living.

After graduating from Southeastern Baptist Theological Seminary in 1996 with his Master of Divinity degree, Scott immediately embarked on a journey of faith and ministry, traveling extensively throughout the United States and abroad. Under the mentorship of Paul E. Tsika (https://www.plowon.org) for over three decades, he has dedicated his life to preaching the gospel and teaching the transformative truths of the Kingdom to those seeking to optimize their walk with God and their life's impact for His glory.

Scott presides over Scott Newton Smith Ministries, Inc. a non-profit 501(c)3 organization, along with his board of directors.

God has opened doors for Scott's dynamic ministry to minister in countless churches, conferences, and student camps, where he passionately delivers messages of hope, revival and victory. He resides near Atlanta, Georgia with his wife, Scarlet, to whom he's been married since 1996. There they they oversee several impactful ministries. These include Branches Lodge, a sanctuary for pastors seeking refreshment and renewal, as well as initiatives aimed at combating sexual exploitation, and spreading the gospel further.

Through his work, Scott aims to equip believers with the tools needed to lead a triumphant Christian life, fostering a deeper connection with God as well as empowering individuals to make a significant impact in their world.

Learn more at www.SNSministries.org.